Developing and Sustaining Sport Psychology Programs

Developing and Sustaining Sport Psychology Programs: A Resource Guide for Practitioners outlines a systemic approach to creating comprehensive, sustainable sport psychology programs in professional sports organizations, colleges, universities, and at secondary school levels.

Based on the author's more than 30 years of professional experience, this volume presents a framework that delineates methods for designing, implementing, and evaluating sport psychology programs, discussing topics such as needs assessment and client identification. Featuring real-world experiences and clear, non-technical writing, this step-by-step guide can be applied to a range of sport psychology programs including mental skills, life skills, coach education, leadership training, and team development programs.

Developing and Sustaining Sport Psychology Programs details a program development process that has been applied successfully at the professional, collegiate, and secondary school levels over a more than 30-year period. It has contributed to the development of sport psychology programs that have sustained themselves over the course of time and is an essential text for sport psychologists and mental skills coaches at all levels as well as graduate students and other professionals in the field.

Charles A. Maher is a Sport and Performance Psychologist and Senior Director of the Department of Personal and Organizational Performance with the Cleveland Indians Baseball Organization.

"Dr. Maher has detailed the sport psychology program development and evaluation techniques that have made him a standout in the highly competitive world of professional sport psychology consulting. The strong theoretical foundation, real-world examples, and professional practice exercises provide key information that novices and professionals in the field are likely to find themselves revisiting again and again. Bravo!"

—*Judy L. Van Raalte, Springfield College, USA*

"Dr. Maher has put together an outstanding innovative resource guide for practitioners that focuses on a systems-based approach to program development and service delivery. There is nothing else like it in the Sport Psychology Literature. The book provides a practical, thorough, systematic framework for designing, planning, implementing, and evaluating tailor made intervention programs that fit the needs of any sport organization and/or team. I highly recommend it!"

—*Dave Yukelson, Association for Applied Sport Psychology, USA*

"Invaluable resource for anyone developing sport psychology programs for individuals, groups, teams, and organizations. Maher has years of experience at all levels of sport, and is ideally suited to present an excellent framework for clarification, design, implementation, and evaluation of successful sport psychology programs."

—*Michael L. Sachs, Temple University, USA*

"This cutting-edge book provides a clear, concise, and practical template for the delivery of valuable sport psychology services to individual athletes, coaches, teams, and organizations. Both seasoned and early career professionals will find this useful in developing programs that will be comprehensive, self-correcting, and sustainable. This is a unique and highly valuable contribution to the field of applied sport psychology."

—*Jack J. Lesyk, Ohio Center for Sport Psychology, USA*

Developing and Sustaining Sport Psychology Programs

A Resource Guide for Practitioners

Charles A. Maher

Routledge
Taylor & Francis Group

NEW YORK AND LONDON

First published 2021
by Routledge
52 Vanderbilt Avenue, New York, NY 10017

and by Routledge
2 Park Square, Milton Park, Abingdon, Oxon, OX14 4RN

Routledge is an imprint of the Taylor & Francis Group, an informa business

Library of Congress Cataloging-in-Publication Data
Names: Maher, Charles A., 1944– author.
Title: Developing and sustaining sport psychology programs: a resource guide for practitioners / Charles A. Maher.
Description: New York, NY : Routledge, 2020. |
Includes bibliographical references and index.
Identifiers: LCCN 2020011188 (print) | LCCN 2020011189 (ebook) |
ISBN 9780367345549 (hardback) | ISBN 9780367345563 (paperback) |
ISBN 9780429326523 (ebook)
Subjects: LCSH: Sports–Psychological aspects. |
Athletes–Mental health services–Planning.
Classification: LCC GV706.4 .M325 2020 (print) |
LCC GV706.4 (ebook) | DDC 796.01–dc23
LC record available at https://lccn.loc.gov/2020011188
LC ebook record available at https://lccn.loc.gov/2020011189

ISBN: 978-0-367-34554-9 (hbk)
ISBN: 978-0-367-34556-3 (pbk)
ISBN: 978-0-429-32652-3 (ebk)

Typeset in Adobe Caslon Pro
by Newgen Publishing UK

CONTENTS

PREFACE

I have been practicing sport and performance psychology for 31 continuous years. I consider myself fortunate to have collaborated with athletes, coaches, teams, and administrators in a range of professional sports franchises, collegiate athletic departments, and other organizational entities during this time. My collaboration has been, and continues to be, focused on addressing the mental and emotional needs of athletes and staff through sport psychology programs. My experiences have confirmed that these programs can be developed in a practical manner and can sustain themselves over the course of time.

This book is about the process that I have created and used in clarifying, designing, implementing, and evaluating sport psychology programs. This process has enriched my overall professional practice, and I have derived considerable professional satisfaction from my engagement in it. With the continued growth of applied sport psychology at professional, collegiate, and even youth sports levels, I believe that the time is right for me to describe this program development process in detail, so that it can be valuable to practitioners.

The process of developing a sport psychology program that has value for program participants and can stand the test of time is not an end unto itself. Rather, the process is applied so that athletes, as well as other target populations such as coaches, can attain goals that contribute to their mental and emotional development, particularly in relation to their performance. In collaboration with others, I have successfully applied this process to a range of sport psychology programs that relate to mental skills, life skills, mental health education, substance abuse prevention, team performance, coach education, executive staff development, and sport services delivery systems.

The impetus for developing sport psychology programs, using a systematic process such as the one covered in this book, is more important now than ever before. Practitioners involved in sport psychology, including me, have witnessed an expansion of requests for sport psychology programs and services. In particular, these requests have been for the design and implementation of programs that are practical, that have value for those who participate in them, and that can sustain themselves over the course of time.

Relatedly, general managers, athletic directors, and other executives who oversee athletes and their development have been increasingly interested in and willing to fund sport psychology programs. However, they desire to know what they are getting for their money as well as how the program can be integrated into the operations of their sport enterprises. More specifically, leaders who work in organizations that are devoted to sports are expecting sport psychology programs to be ones that actually can be implemented. In the real-time contexts of their organizations, these administrators want programs that can remain in operation, especially given the constraints under which their departments and units operate.

This book is a resource intended to guide professionals—perhaps including you—who are involved in the practice of sport psychology to learn how to develop programs that can be designed and implemented in real-time sports-related organizations and settings.

The program development process you will learn about in this book consists of four phases: Clarification, Design, Implementation, and Evaluation. This book discusses the purpose of each phase and includes steps, methods, and procedures. Each phase will be illustrated with real-life examples and coupled with practitioner exercises.

The process for developing and sustaining a sport psychology program that you will learn about in this book adheres to four criteria. I have found these criteria to be important in my work as a sport and performance psychologist. I have relied on these criteria in making sure the process will lead to programs that can add value to athletes, coaches, and other stakeholders.

These four criteria are:

- *Practicality* – The process allows for the design and implementation of a program that is capable of being implemented in sports organizations and related organizational settings and that has the potential to remain in operation in the respective organization.
- *Utility* – The process leads to the generation of information that will assist practitioners in deciding how to move ahead with developing a program, how to keep it in operation, or how to curtail its development and continuation.
- *Propriety* – The process seeks to ensure that the program is designed and implemented in ways that take into consideration ethical standards as well as the relevant characteristics of the athletes and others who will be participating in the program.
- *Technical Defensibility* – The process places a premium on the use of program planning, evaluation methods, and procedures that are practical and appropriate for both the particular program development task at hand and the context in which the program is being designed and implemented.

ORGANIZATION OF THE BOOK

The book is organized into five separate yet interrelated sections, with each section comprising several chapters.

The initial section of the book is referred to as *Foundations*. The four chapters in this section provide perspectives, principles, and guidelines that set the tone for the use of the program development process in sport psychology. These chapters include steps that need to be taken before you actually initiate the work of developing a sport psychology program.

The next section of the book covers the first of the four phases of the program development process—the *Clarification Phase*. This phase is guided by the principle of knowing why a program is necessary and where it will occur. The phase reflects the belief that before a program can be designed, the sport psychology-related needs of program participants should be assessed within the cultural and organizational context in which those needs are embedded. More specifically, you will learn to examine the unique needs of those who will participate in the program in the real-time context.

The ensuing section of the book covers the second phase of the process—the *Design Phase*. The principle associated with this phase states that before a program is implemented, it is necessary to document the design of that program. That is, you must create a full picture of the program and create relevant documentation; otherwise, it will not be clear what is going to be implemented. This documentation should include the purpose and goals of the program, the program's organization, and the "evaluability" of the program.

The subsequent section of the book deals with the third phase of the process—the *Implementation Phase*. The principle on which this phase rests states that once a program has been designed—yet before it can be evaluated—it is necessary to ascertain how the program actually has been implemented. Through the chapters covered in this section, you will be taught how to monitor the extent to which the program has been implemented according to its program design. You will also learn how to discern what situations signal the necessity for adjustments while the program is in operation.

The final section of the book involves the fourth phase of the process—the *Evaluation Phase*. This phase is informed by the principle that in order to make evaluative judgments about the program, following its implementation, it is best to have a program evaluation plan in place. This plan specifies program evaluation questions, data collection methods, and related procedures. This phase is crucial in deciding how the program can be continued, further developed, and sustained in your particular organization.

I have applied all of the guidelines and materials that will be presented in this book—perspectives, principles, phases, steps, methods, procedures, examples, and case illustrations—in real-time sports organizations, particularly at the professional and collegiate levels. I have done so over the course of many years, either alone or in collaboration with others. This book offers a proven, time-tested process to help you and the organizations with which you work develop a valuable sport psychology program.

Here is a flow chart of the sport psychology program development process:

Figure P.1 Four phases of the sport psychology program development process.

PHILOSOPHY OF SPORT PSYCHOLOGY PROGRAM DEVELOPMENT

Before proceeding, however, I want to describe my professional philosophy about the process of developing sport psychology programs that have value and that can sustain themselves in sport organizations and other organizations. Without a doubt, my philosophy of sport psychology program development has influenced my overall professional practice, including the information presented in this book.

My philosophy of sport psychology program development reflects the following beliefs:

1. Sport psychology is an area of theory, research, and practice that can be placed under the larger domain of performance psychology.

2. In terms of professional practice, sport psychology programs can be considered as the work and actions undertaken by practitioners that are intended to assist athletes and others with the enhancement of mental and emotional development, especially in relation to competitive performance.

3. Given this concept, sport psychology programs can be developed for athletes, coaches, and teams, as well as larger departmental and organizational units, at youth sports, secondary school, collegiate, and professional levels.

4. One major category of sport psychology practice is that of the design, implementation, and evaluation of a sport psychology program, which is the focus of this book.

5. I define a sport psychology program as an organized configuration of resources—human, technological, informational, physical, and financial—that are customized and intended to enable athletes or other participants to attain one or more goals associated with mental and emotional development, with particular reference to competitive performance, within a program embedded in relevant social, cultural, and organizational contexts.

6. There are no "cookie-cutter" sport psychology programs. A sport psychology program may be big or small, specific to a few athletes or many athletes, focused on the needs of coaches and other staff, or targeting a component of a larger organizational service delivery system. The nature and scope of any particular program will depend on what is possible given the context, available information, and current understanding of the context.

7. The application of a systematic process for developing the program is a useful investment of time and effort for all concerned. Such application increases the likelihood that a sport psychology program will contribute to the mental and emotional development and performance of athletes and that it will sustain itself in the organization if it is determined to have value for program participants.

8. A process that can increase the likelihood of developing a valuable and sustainable sport psychology program involves application of the following: (a) *clarifying* the participants for the program, their mental and emotional development needs, and the relevant context in which those needs are embedded; (b) *designing* the program in an organized manner, based on needs and context assessment information; (c) *implementing* the program according to its design, while making necessary adjustments once the program is implemented; and (d) *evaluating* the program in a practical and informative way, so that decisions can be made about how to continue to develop and improve the program.

9. There are many types of programs that I consider as sport psychology programs. These programs are those associated with mental skills, life skills, mental health, substance abuse prevention, coach

education, staff development, team performance, administration and supervision of sport psychology services, and organizational development.

10. In order to provide program development services in the area of sport psychology, I need to hold myself accountable that I am practicing within the bounds of my competence, which is based on my education, training, supervised experience, licensure, and certifications.

11. I adhere to the ethics codes of the American Psychological Association and the Association of Applied Sport Psychology.

In closing this preface to the book, I want to emphasize the following: A mental performance coach or sport psychologist, practicing within the bounds of their professional competence, can learn to apply the guidelines contained in this book for developing and sustaining sport psychology programs. This intention is reflected by the following statement:

> Give a sport psychology practitioner a program, and they will implement it for a day. Teach the practitioner how to develop sport psychology programs using a systematic process, and they will have a professional competency that will last them a lifetime.

Through the guidelines in this book, I hope you will be able to identify many opportunities to develop sport psychology programs that are valuable and sustainable and that add value to your clients and to your practice.

Charles A. Maher, PsyD, FAASP, CMPC
Cleveland, Ohio
April 2020

ACKNOWLEDGMENTS

I would like to thank my wife, Ann, for her continued love and support, including her patience and understanding, as I authored this book. I also want to thank the many professional and collegiate athletes, coaches, and support staffs who have participated in the sport psychology programs on which this book is based: your participation has taught me a great deal about designing, implementing, and evaluating sport psychology programs. Finally, and very importantly, I appreciate the assistance of Sandy Haney, who has served as my editorial advisor for this book. Without Sandy's cogent suggestions, attention to detail, and timeliness, this book would not have come to fruition.

PART I
FOUNDATIONS

Taking a Systems Perspective on Sport Psychology
Defining and Illustrating Sport Psychology Programs
Setting the Stage for Program Development
Overviewing the Program Development Process

1

TAKING A SYSTEMS PERSPECTIVE ON SPORT PSYCHOLOGY

The purpose of this chapter is to provide a systems perspective on sport psychology, which will serve as backdrop to the sport psychology program development process covered in this book. It is the systems perspective that I have relied on when designing, implementing, and evaluating sport psychology programs in professional sport settings, college athletic departments, and other organizations. Accordingly, I will present a systems framework as a practical means of focusing on and engaging in the program development process—at individual, group, team, and organizational levels.

During my many years of practicing sport and performance psychology, one thing has become increasingly clear to me: sport psychology has many dimensions to it, besides intervening with the individual athlete (Raaen & Mugford, 2019). Depending on one's role and point of view, sport psychology can be considered as a professional discipline, a body of research-informed knowledge, and/or an area of service delivery, among other considerations (Aoyagi & Portenga, 2010).

In this book, I will be defining sport psychology as a professional discipline whose intention is to add value to a range of clients and program participants. This range includes, of course, athletes, but it also is of value to coaches, athletic trainers, strength and conditioning specialists, teams, general managers, and executives, as well as entire sports organizations.

However, in order for sport psychology to provide value to this wide range of clients and program participants, a systems perspective is key. I have found this to be true in my professional practice, and I want to share that perspective here.

Nature of a Systems Perspective

A systems perspective on sport psychology, as I am framing it, allows the practitioner the opportunity to place sport psychology programs within the larger social, cultural, competitive, and organizational contexts (Wagstaff, 2017). More basically, a systems perspective on sport psychology highlights opportunities for the practitioner to develop programs at many different levels of sports organizations and related organizations.

Without a systems perspective on professional practice, the practitioner and others will not identify opportunities for the development of sport psychology programs in sports organizations and related organizations. Thus, practical ways for making contributions, beyond providing individual interventions for individual athletes, will go unrecognized and unrealized (Checkland, 1999).

A Systems Framework for Program Development in Sport Psychology

With respect to deciding what, whether, and how to design and implement sport psychology programs for my clients, I use the following framework. It is derived from a systems perspective and is represented as a table in Table 1.1. This framework has guided my program development work.

This systems framework consists of three constituent dimensions. These are:

1. *Level of Service Delivery* – seen as the vertical dimension of the framework.
2. *Program Development Process* – seen as the horizontal dimension of the framework.
3. *Methods and Procedures* – seen as the matrix cells.

Level of Service Delivery

This vertical dimension of the framework highlights the reality that sport psychology programs can be provided at various levels, and also to different

Table 1.1 Systems framework for program development in sport psychology

	Clarification	Design	Implementation	Evaluation
Individual				
Group				
Team				
Organizational				

people at each level, with regard to mental and emotional development and performance. These levels are:

- *Individual Level* – This level serves to identify opportunities for programs for one athlete at a time. At this level, the program is commonly referred to as an athlete intervention. Typically, this has been the thrust of many sport psychology programs, although the term "program" often has not been used at this level.
- *Group Level* – This level serves to identify opportunities for programs for a group of athletes or coaches, such as all players on the defensive unit of an American football team or all assistant coaches of a basketball team. At this level, the program also could address the performance or personal needs of each particular group.
- *Team Level* – This level serves to identify opportunities for programs for a team of athletes or to an entire performance team. At this level, the program is often referred to as a team development program.
- *Organizational Level* – This level serves to identify opportunities for programs that encompass a large number of athletes, staffs, and executives. At this level, these programs often are referred to as a sport psychology service delivery system or an organizational development program.

Program Development Process

The horizontal dimension of the systems framework depicts the process that I have used in developing sport psychology programs at each level of service delivery. This dimension emphasizes that although the level of service delivery will vary by level, the process is the same across levels. The detailed description and application of this process will be reflected by the guidelines that will be presented in this book.

The four phases of the sport psychology program development process are:

- *Clarification* – This phase involves identifying and describing the participants for the program. It considers how the program can address participants' mental and emotional needs and gives attention to the context in which those needs are embedded.
- *Design* – This phase involves describing the purpose and goals of the program, as well as the organization of the program, so that the goals will be attained and the program can be evaluated.
- *Implementation* – This phase involves making sure that the program is being implemented as designed, while making necessary adjustments so that the program will sustain itself.
- *Evaluation* – This phase involves determining the extent to which the program has been considered as being valuable to program participants. Similarly, it considers whether and to what extent the program should be continued.

Methods and Procedures

This is the third dimension of the systems framework. It is the intersection of the Level of Service Delivery and Program Development Process dimensions.

Each cell of the matrix refers to the types of methods and procedures that are used at each phase of the process. Furthermore, the matrix cells also serve to illustrate that, although the process of program development is the same for any of the levels, the methods and procedures will be different. For instance, the methods and procedures used to clarify, design, implement, and evaluate a sport psychology program at the team level will be different than those methods and procedures used at the individual or organizational level.

Professional Practice Exercises

At the conclusion of each chapter of the book, I will provide you with some exercises that you may want to engage in and that may be useful in your own work in developing sport psychology programs. These exercises may also help you learn about yourself with regard to that task.

For this current chapter, consider the following questions:

1. What kinds of sport psychology programs have you been involved with as a practitioner?

2. How have you endeavored to identify opportunities that allow you to develop sport psychology programs?
3. To what types of populations of athletes or others have you been able to target your programs?
4. What has gone well or not so well with your work in those programmatic areas? What have you learned from them?
5. In what ways might the systems framework, as described in this chapter, assist you in your work?

2

DEFINING AND ILLUSTRATING SPORT PSYCHOLOGY PROGRAMS

The purpose of this chapter is to consider the definition of a sport psychology program. This understanding will help you decide what a sport psychology program can be and how to proceed to develop one. In addition to defining terms, I will provide examples of programs that meet this definition. Most of these examples will be of sport psychology programs that I have developed and helped to sustain over time, both alone and with others. Finally, this chapter delineates the quality indicators for determining whether a sport psychology program is valuable and sustainable.

Defining a Sport Psychology Program

There is no consistent definition of a sport psychology program, in terms of programs that occur in real-time organizations, at least as far as I am aware. Therefore, it is not surprising that the term "sport psychology program" will mean different things to different people (Poczwardowski & Sherman, 2011).

However, when the task turns to developing a valuable and sustainable sport psychology program, it is important to understand what you mean by the term "program." Otherwise, without this clarification, those concerned—athletes, coaches, general managers, athletic administrators, or other stakeholders—will not have a clear sense of what is to be developed. Moreover, opportunities for developing a sport psychology program may be lost, since the nature of a program needs to be recognized by clients who will be involved with the program's design and implementation (Keegan, 2015).

Here is the definition of a sport psychology program that has proven useful to me and to colleagues when talking with clients about programs and their development:

A Sport Psychology Program is an organized configuration of resources, intended to contribute to the mental and emotional development of athletes and others in the sport community, as performers and people.

Let us analyze this definition and look at its essential elements:

- *Organized Configuration of Resources* – In order to design and implement a sport psychology program, a range of resources is essential (Heath & Heath, 2007). Without the availability of particular resources, a sports organization will not develop and sustain a program. These resources include *human resources* (athletes, coaches, and program staff), *informational resources* (program purpose and goals), *technological resources* (methods and procedures), *financial resources* (budget), and *physical resources* (facilities, equipment).
- *Mental and Emotional Development* – The intention of most sport psychology programs is to assist athletes in developing skills so that they can use their thoughts, emotions, and actions for consistent, successful performance. This is what I refer to as mental and emotional development. This development can be measured/seen in numerous ways. Athletes' use of productive *thoughts*, *emotions*, and *actions* will be evident in how they prepare for competition and how consistent they are at focusing on the task at hand while competing. Their response to their results and their use of performance feedback, as well as how they balance the demands of their sports with the rest of their lives, will also demonstrate their development.
- *Performers and People* – Many, if not most, sport psychology programs are concerned with how the program has contributed to the performance of athletes. In addition, sport performance includes how the athletes have developed as people as well as how coaches have fulfilled their roles and responsibilities (Maher, 2018). In this regard,

performance is demonstrated through the ways individuals and teams respond to competition. Personal development is apparent when athletes and others make healthy choices and effective decisions.

Illustrations of Real-Time Sport Psychology Programs

According to the definition of a sport psychology program provided above, I have been very fortunate to have been involved in the design, implementation, and evaluation of many sport psychology programs over the years, both as a sport and performance psychologist and as a program consultant.

In order to illustrate the range of programs that can be considered sport psychology programs, I want to give brief descriptions of some of these programs. Most of these programs have been determined as being valuable, based on their purposes and goals, by their organizations.

These examples are not ranked in any order of importance, nor are they intended to be detailed program designs or evaluation reports. Rather, they simply provide summarized examples of such programs. Most of these example programs have been implemented and sustained over the course of time, including some programs that have lasted for many years.

Moreover, it is important to note here that in order to adhere to confidentiality and proprietary requirements, I do not include specific names of the organizations and people involved in these programs.

- *Mental Skills Program for Division I Student-Athletes* – This program was divided into three sections: one targeted football players in one program section, one men's basketball players, and yet another women's basketball players. The program was designed so that players could acquire and develop mental skills that would allow them to: (a) prepare for competition in a quality way; (b) compete with a mind in the moment presence; and (c) engage in accurate self-evaluation of their performance. The program was implemented over the course of a calendar year, before, during, and after the respective competitive seasons.
- *Mental Foundations Program for Professional Baseball Players* – This program targeted players from the United States and Latin American countries who were in their first season of playing professional baseball. The program was designed to assist these players to learn about themselves as people and as performers, as well as to

learn to balance baseball effectively with the rest of their lives. The program was implemented during the spring training time period of the baseball year.

- *Performance Enhancement Program for an NBA Team* – This program targeted all players on a team that competed in the National Basketball Association (NBA). It was implemented during the course of a season and focused on assisting players to develop and use mental and emotional skills to cope with the range of demands that they encountered during the season. It particularly addressed dealing effectively with people, places, and things that could derail their seasons and careers.
- *Rookie Level Mental Skills Program for an NFL Team* – This program targeted players with less than two years of experience playing for a National Football League (NFL) team. Through the program, the players were instructed how to use a set of mental criteria and taught how to monitor themselves in relation to those criteria throughout the season.
- *Sport Psychology Education Program for High School Student-Athletes* – This program targeted student-athletes in a large public high school in the Northeastern United States who were in their junior and senior years. As part of a year-long course, sport psychology graduate student interns educated the student-athletes about the field of sport psychology as well as about how to develop and use basic mental skills for performance and personal development purposes.
- *Cultural Transition Program for an MLB Organization* – In this program, young international players who had recently signed to be a member of this Major League Baseball (MLB) organization were provided year-long instruction to help them transition in an effective manner from the Dominican Republic to the United States and its professional baseball culture. As a component of the program, players and staff in the United States were taught how to understand and relate to these new players, particularly as the international players transitioned to the United States and to rookie ball teams in the organization.
- *Mental Skill Rehabilitation Program for Professional Baseball Players* – This program targeted minor and major league players from an MLB organization who were undergoing physical rehabilitation of longstanding and chronic injuries. In particular, the program focused

on teaching and guiding players to use mental skills to cope with and enhance their physical rehabilitation.

- *Coach Education Program for Division I Athletic Coaches* – This program targeted all head coaches and assistant coaches of all sports at a Division I university. The program was designed so that the coaches could learn both about the mental and emotional development of their players and about how to teach mental skills to their players. The program was implemented in planned sessions over the course of the year.

- *Mental Health Screening Program for Division II Student-Athletes* – This program targeted student-athletes in several sports at a Division II university. As part of the pre-participation assessment process, student-athletes completed a form about how they cope with stress and other challenges. The players then had one-on-one meetings with the sport psychologist to discuss their responses.

- *Team Development Program for a Women's Swimming and Diving Team* – This program targeted all team members over the course of a season. The program was designed to instruct and guide the players in communicating and collaborating with one another, both in and out of the pool.

Indicators of a Valuable and Sustainable Sport Psychology Program

Since this is a book about developing valuable and sustainable sport psychology programs, I want to define what I mean when I talk about a program that can be implemented in the real time of sports organizations and other organizations such as educational institutions. That is, I want to describe to you a program that has value in those settings, for athletes and for others.

In essence, I label a sport psychology program "valuable and sustainable" when it is an organized configuration of resources in which the following conditions exist. First, it assesses important mental and emotional development needs of athletes, with particular reference to performance. In addition, the program has been designed in a way so that it can actually be implemented in a particular organizational setting. Furthermore, there is evidence that the program has contributed to the attainment of program goals, that there have been positive reactions to the program, and that there is a desire to keep the program in operation and possibly to expand it.

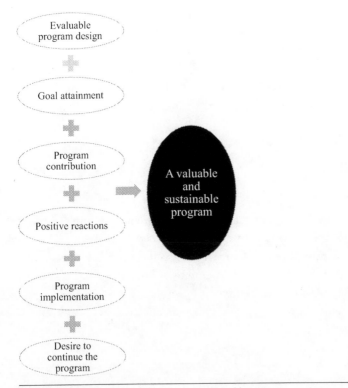

Figure 2.1 Six indicators of a valuable and sustainable program.

Within this context, there are six indicators of an effective and sustainable program. These indicators were present in the programs that I described above in this chapter and are visually portrayed in Figure 2.1. These indicators are:

1. *Evaluable Program Design* – There is a written description of the program that allows for monitoring of its implementation, in order to track if the program has been implemented as designed.
2. *Goal Attainment* – The target population for the program—athletes or others—has made progress toward the outcome goals of the program.
3. *Program Contribution* – There are informed opinions that the program did occur and that the program has contributed to the attainment of the outcome goals of the program.
4. *Positive Reactions* – Participants in the program as well as others who have a stake in it have reacted positively to the program.

5. *Program Implementation* – The program has been implemented in a practical way, with appropriate use of resources, without undue disruption to the operational routines of the organization.

6. *Desire to Continue the Program* – The program has been judged as being worth the investment of resources and as worth continuing or perhaps even being implemented at another site.

Professional Practice Exercises

In terms of material covered in this chapter, consider the following exercises and activities:

1. What kinds of programs have you designed and implemented? How did you proceed with these tasks or possibilities?

2. Have you missed or failed to recognize opportunities to design and implement sport psychology programs? Why? What can you learn from that missed opportunity?

3. What does the task of developing an effective sport psychology program mean to you?

3

SETTING THE STAGE FOR PROGRAM DEVELOPMENT

The purpose of this chapter is to review steps that should be taken before you begin to engage in the process of developing a sport psychology program. The ensuing chapters of the book will cover the process in detail.

The preliminary steps covered in this current chapter will help you set the stage for applying the program development process. I have found that engaging in these steps increases the likelihood of establishing and maintaining a professional and productive relationship with your client, as well as with other individuals who will be involved in the sport program development process.

These steps are:

- Adhere to an ethical stance.
- Identify your client for program development.
- Clarify your role with your client.
- Determine the motivation of your client.
- Explain the program development task.
- Describe the program development process.
- Formulate a written agreement with the client.
- Follow through with the written agreement.

Here is a visual picture of these steps.

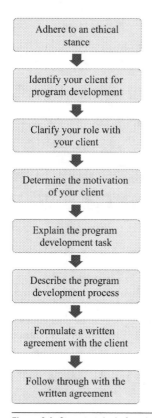

Figure 3.1 Steps to take before developing a sport psychology program.

Adhere to an Ethical Stance

As practitioners, we are expected to abide by a code of professional ethics. Adherence to a code of ethics serves as a basis for making decisions about the nature and scope of our professional practice—and the work of developing sport psychology programs is no exception to such an expectation. In this regard, the code of ethics of the American Psychological Association and the code of ethics of the Association of Applied Sport Psychology help us perform our work ethically.

With regard to the process of developing sport psychology programs, and assuming that we desire to take an ethical stance, the following areas are of utmost importance: (a) practicing within the bounds of one's professional competence; (b) providing necessary assurances of confidentiality to athletes and others; (c) understanding the culture and ethnicity of athletes, coaches, and others who will be involved in sport psychology programs; and (d) using only psychological and educational tests and measurements for which you have received proper training.

Identify Your Client for Program Development

The term "client," as I have used in this book and in my own professional practice, has a specific meaning. A "client" for program development in sport psychology is the individual in a sports organization, athletic department, or other organizational entity with whom you will communicate and collaborate as you engage in the process of program development.

Depending on the nature and scope of the sport psychology program to be developed, your client may be one of the following:

- *Yourself* – You are the client if you function in a role such as director of a department of mental performance or in another relevant director or coordinator position.
- *Coach of an Athletic Team* – Your client may be a head coach or an assistant coach who is interested in the mental and emotional development and performance of the athletes who are part of their team.
- *Athletic Director or General Manager* – Your client may be the individual who oversees and directs all sport-related programs and services and who wants to build sport psychology programs into their department or their unit of operations.
- *Director of a Sports Medicine Department* – This is a client who has responsibility to make sure that sport psychology programs are provided in a way that is integrated with other performance and medical services.
- *Other* – Your client may include other individuals who have a direct stake in the development of sport psychology programs.

Clarify Your Role with Your Client

Before anything else, you need to make clear your role in the program development process to your client as well as to all others who will be involved with you in developing a sport psychology program (Maher & Taylor, 2015). If you are unclear about your role in the development process, communication may be limited with your client, and others may likely misconstrue the nature and scope of your involvement.

Your role in the sport psychology program development process may be one of the following:

- *External Consultant* – In this role, you are not employed by the organization. Rather, you are a professional who is external to it, such as a sport psychologist or a mental performance consultant. As an external consultant, you typically are asked to assist in the development of a sport psychology program, often as part of a program development committee or team, in a particular organizational context that is related to sport.
- *Director of an Athletic Department or Player Development Coordinator* – In this role, you are employed by the organization in a director or coordinator role. In such a role, you want to make sure that you design and implement a program that enhances the mental and emotional development of athletes in relation to their performance and personal development.
- *Mental Performance Coach* – In this role, you also are an employee of an organization. In the role of a mental performance coach, you desire to take the initiative to make sure that whatever sport psychology program is designed is one that addresses and prioritizes the mental and emotional needs of athletes.
- *Other* – You may also serve in another type of relevant role, depending on circumstances and context.

Clarifying your role is a key step, since knowledge of your role in relation to the development of a sport psychology program is important for your client, as well as for the coaches, administrators, and athletes who have a stake in the program.

Determine the Motivation of Your Client

This step involves getting to know your client so that you can learn what specifically they desire or are interested in with respect to the development of a sport psychology program (Sharp & Hodge, 2011). During this step, it will be useful to learn why they contacted you to ascertain their particular intentions.

In my professional experiences, many things may motivate a client to work with you. Some predominant reasons are reflected in the following real-life scenarios:

- *Scenario 1* – Someone in an authority position in the organization, such as your client's supervisor, has requested that a sport psychology program be developed and become operational. In this scenario, your client is motivated to follow the orders of their supervisor.
- *Scenario 2* – Your client desires to provide their athletes with opportunities so that they can gain a competitive edge with their performance.
- *Scenario 3* – Your client feels that a mental skills program will be a positive offering for their athletes and their organization.
- *Scenario 4* – Your client believes that the mental side of sport is an important aspect, and they want their athletes to develop their mental game.
- *Scenario 5* – Your client would like to develop a sport psychology program that is similar to programs they have heard about or encountered in other sports organizations.

Explain the Program Development Task

You should not overlook the critical importance of explaining the task of developing a sport psychology program. That is, the program development task at hand involves being clear to your client and all concerned about what you will do and how you will proceed in program development activities such as needs assessment, goal setting, implementation, and program evaluation (Maher, 2012). You should make clear to your client and others that the task aims to develop a program that will benefit athletes or other target populations, such as coaches. You should also clarify that the program will be implemented in a way that does not allow for undue disruption to operational routines of the organization.

Relatedly, it needs to be made clear to all concerned that the task of program development is not one of applied research or related research activities. Although applied research is an important aspect of sport psychology, it is not the path to take if there is interest in developing and sustaining a sport psychology program at the present time, in your particular context, for specific athletes who are likely to be the participants of the program. In other words, the task of program development prioritizes program development for a particular group of athletes in a specific context: it is customized to their needs, rather than focusing on hypothesis testing or theory development.

Explain the Program Development Process

Explaining the process you will take in developing the program—such as the process covered in this book—has many benefits. It will help your client understand not only what you are going to do, but also why it is important to develop a program in a systematic manner. It will also define how you will proceed in working with them. More specifically, your explanation should include discussion with your client about what it will take to clarify the need for their program and how to proceed with its design, implementation, and evaluation (Taylor, 2008).

Furthermore, an explanation of your program development process will enable your client to learn about how you function as a professional and what you consider to be important with regard to the program development task.

Formulate a Written Agreement with Your Client

This step solidifies the agreement between you and your client, given your role in program development. This agreement may be in the form of a memorandum of agreement, a more formal and written contract, or another type of document, depending on the organization and context (Maher & Taylor, 2015). The agreement should not be a verbal one, since a verbal agreement leaves too much to chance, including what kind of program is to be developed.

No matter what form a written agreement with your client takes, the essentials of the document should include the following:

- Overview and purpose of the agreement.
- The program development task to be accomplished.
- The process that you will use in the accomplishment of the task.
- The information and documents that will be delivered and to whom this material will be provided.
- Staff who will be involved in the process.
- Timelines.
- Budget and compensation.

Follow Through With the Written Agreement

This step involves making a commitment to yourself and to your client to follow through with your part of the agreement. Depending on the particular agreement, your subsequent actions may include clarifying the need for the program, designing a program based on needs and context assessment, implementing the program, and evaluating it.

Professional Practice Exercises

1. Think back on the steps you have taken in your prior work with planning sport psychology programs. What did you do well that solidified your role with your client? Did you have challenges in identifying and learning about the client?

2. What kinds of memoranda of agreement or contracts have you developed when involved in the task of developing programs? To what extent have they been satisfied or useful? If you did not develop any, what was the reason for not doing so?

3. What do you want to repeat and what do you want to change, based on your answers to questions 1 and 2, as you think about next steps in your sport psychology work?

4
OVERVIEWING THE PROGRAM
DEVELOPMENT PROCESS

This chapter outlines the four phases of the process for developing and sustaining a sport psychology program. It also describes the steps of each of its phases. Later chapters will provide detail and more information regarding each step. This overview of the phases and their steps will help you place the steps of each of the four phases within the bigger picture of the sport psychology program development process.

Phases of the Program Development Process

The sport psychology program development process includes four separate, yet interrelated, phases. By engaging in these phases in a step-by-step manner, you increase the likelihood that the sport psychology program you develop will be customized to the needs and contexts of the athletes as well as others who will be involved in the program. In addition, by using the phases in a step-by-step manner, the program you develop will have an increased likelihood of adding value to those who participate in it. Furthermore, the chances increase that the program will sustain itself over the course of time (Maher, 2012).

The phases of the sport psychology program development process are the following:

Phase 1: Clarification Phase – determining the reason for a program.

Phase 2: Design Phase – organizing the program so that it can be implemented.

Phase 3: Implementation Phase – monitoring how the program is operating.

Phase 4: Evaluation Phase – making judgments about the value of the program.

Figure 4.1 is a visual portrayal of the sport psychology program development process. The figure serves to illustrate that the phases, although separate, are interrelated. The figure also reveals that the information from one phase builds on information from the prior phase and that information from the Evaluation Phase feeds back into the Design Phase and the Clarification Phases.

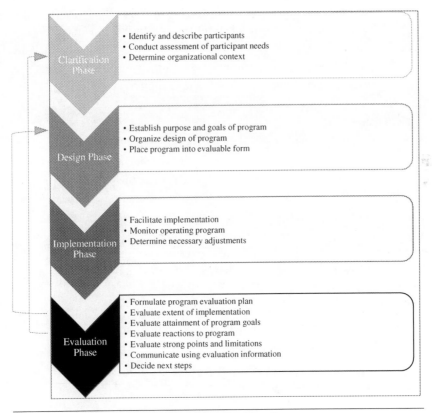

Figure 4.1 Phases of the sport psychology program development process.

Clarification Phase

Before you can design a sport psychology program, it is necessary to decide if there should be one in the first place. Without clarification about the reason for a program, it will be difficult to design one that will have value for its participants. Relatedly, it will be hard for the program to be able to sustain itself once it has been implemented (Kaufman, 2000). Therefore, the purpose of the Clarification Phase is to identify both why a sport psychology program is necessary in the first place and for whom the program is intended.

The steps for successful application of the Clarification Phase are:

1. Identify and describe who will be participating in the program, such as a particular team or group of athletes.
2. Conduct an assessment of the mental and emotional needs of the intended program participants, particularly in relation to their performance demands.
3. Determine the organizational context in which the mental and emotional needs of the target population are embedded. This includes matters pertaining to culture and ethnicity, as well as linguistic, social, and systemic factors (Brown, Gould, & Foster, 2015).

Design Phase

Once you have clarified the reason for a sport psychology program, it is then appropriate to design the program. You, your client, and other relevant stakeholders, including participants, will know what the program represents and how it will be implemented based on the information you provide about the design of the program—that is, what the program comprises. The purpose of the Design Phase is to create a program that has the capacity to be implemented and evaluated, and to be sustainable, within the relevant organizational context.

The steps for the Design Phase are:

1. Establish the purpose and goals of the program.
2. Organize the design of the program in terms of components, sequence, methods, procedures, and activities so that it is capable of being implemented.
3. Place the program into an evaluable form, so that its implementation and outcomes can be evaluated.

Implementation Phase

Before you can evaluate a sport psychology program, you need to determine the extent to which the program has actually occurred. Otherwise, it will not be clear to you, your client, and others whether the program has transpired according to how it was designed. In addition, no one will know if adjustments should be made to the program, including while it is occurring. The purpose of the Implementation Phase is to facilitate the implementation of the program and then monitor how the program is operating following its implementation.

The steps for the Implementation Phase are:

1. Facilitate the implementation of the program.
2. Monitor the extent to which the program is operating according to its program design.
3. Decide whether adjustments are necessary in the program, based on how the program is transpiring.

Evaluation Phase

Before you can make decisions about the continued development and improvement of a sport psychology program, you must make sound judgments about the value of the program for those who have participated in it as well as for the organization in which the program is embedded. Otherwise, it will not be clear what to do next with the program, such as whether to continue it, make adjustments in it, or terminate it. The purpose of the Evaluation Phase is to decide how valuable the program has been for those athletes or others who have participated in the program and then to ascertain what to do next with the program.

The steps for the Evaluation Phase are:

1. Formulate a program evaluation plan, so that data collection and related evaluation activities can occur in a practical and meaningful way.
2. Evaluate the extent of the implementation of the program.
3. Evaluate the degree to which the goals of the program have been attained.
4. Evaluate reactions to the program from those who have participated in it as well as from other relevant stakeholders.

5. Evaluate the strong points and limitations of the program.
6. Communicate and use evaluation information about the program.
7. Decide what to do next with the program.

Professional Practice Exercises

1. As an external sport psychology consultant, you are requested by an athletic director of large high school to implement a mental skills program for all of their student-athletes. How would you proceed in the consideration of this request?
2. What have been the factors that have helped you provide sport psychology programs to date in your professional work? What factors have limited or otherwise curtailed your program development work?
3. How can you handle resistance of clients and others to their involvement in the program development process?

PART II
CLARIFICATION PHASE

Specifying the Program Participants
Assessing the Needs of Program Participants
Determining Relevant Organizational Context

5

SPECIFYING THE PROGRAM PARTICIPANTS

The purpose of this chapter is to provide guidelines about the first step of the Clarification Phase. This first step involves specifying the athletes or others who will be participating in a sport psychology program. This chapter also will provide a rationale for this step, delineate how to obtain the best information possible about program participants, and explain how to present and use that information as part of the process.

Potential Program Participants

The term "program participants" is one that I have used when developing a sport psychology program; I use it in a very purposeful way. "Program participants" refers to the range of athletes or others (e.g., coaches) who may be candidates for involvement in a program. This involvement, of course, assumes that a need exists for a program (see Chapter 6) and that the context indicates the readiness of the organization for a program (see Chapter 7). Accordingly, we cannot assume that all members of a particular target population in a specific setting will participate in a program. Rather, factors such as the size and scope of the program, or other matters such as scheduling issues, will determine the actual target population.

Within the sport psychology program development process, program participants are not the "client." Rather, the client is the individual with whom you will be collaborating as part of the program development process, such as a coach or an athletic director (covered in Chapter 3). The participants of the program include those who actually will be involved in the program.

Examples of participants in sport psychology programs that I have developed are the following:

- 12 members of a women's collegiate basketball team, excluding new arrivals to the team.
- 89 student-athletes in their junior and senior year in a large public high school.
- 9 players, both offensive and defensive, who are being treated for long-term physical injuries in a professional football organization.
- 24 minor league coaches and instructors in a professional baseball organization.
- 10 executive administrators of a state-wide interscholastic association.
- 40 baseball players who are on the 40-man roster of a Major League Baseball team.

Rationale for Specifying Program Participants

Although it may be easy to assume that you and your client know about the athletes who will be participating in a sport psychology program, it is not enough just to know who those athletes are (Brown et al., 2015). Thus, I do not recommend you assume that you understand who these athletes are. Do not skip over this step.

There are several reasons why it is important to specify the participants for a sport psychology program. These reasons are:

- You can document the exact number of athletes who may benefit from participation in a sport psychology program. Such documentation informs you and your client about the size and scope of a program, including possible costs for the program.
- You can make comparisons about the relevant characteristics of the participants of the program (e.g., years of experience in the sport; gender; ethnicity; linguistic proficiency) in relation to any requirements or criteria that may have relevance for their eligibility for a program (e.g., resident of the school district; grade point average).

- As part of a program evaluation, you can make comparisons between those who have participated in the program and those who have not participated in it.
- You can address concerns about the dissemination of an implemented program to other sports and to other contexts and whether those athletes in another setting are similar to those athletes who have participated in the program.

Determining the Number of Potential Program Participants

There are three methods that you can use to determine the potential size and scope of those who will participate in a sport psychology program. These methods are:

- Interview
- Permanent Product Review
- Questionnaire.

Interview

The interview method is a direct way of learning from your client about the size and scope of potential program participants (Fried & Flake, 2018). Through the interview method, you want your client or their designee to provide answers to the following two questions:

- In order to decide how to proceed in developing a sport psychology program, how many athletes would you like to participate in a program?
- Why?

While using the interview method, it sometimes may not be clear to your client what the size or the number of program participants will be. If so, you should encourage your client to make an informed estimate of the size of the group and to explain the rationale for this estimate.

Permanent Product Review

The permanent product review method for determining the potential number of program participants can be used under the following two conditions:

- When there is likely to be a large number of athletes in the target population but the actual number is not apparent.
- When the data to answer the question already exist in a database.

In reviewing permanent product data, you need to consider the reliability of the data. You need to make an informed judgment about this matter, and you may very well have to rely on the opinion of your client or others such as coaches, support staff, or those in the analytics area.

Questionnaire

It is appropriate to consider using a questionnaire to determine the number of potential program participants under the following conditions: (a) when it is not clear how many athletes may be part of the target population; and (b) when the potential program participants may be located over more than one geographic area or organizational site.

When using the questionnaire method, you should consider including the following on your questionnaire:

- You can use a cover letter or message to inform the client (or the designee of the client) that the questionnaire will help identify the number of athletes who may be part of the sport psychology program being considered for development.
- Then, specific items on the questionnaire are:
  - Number of athletes.
  - Whether this number is an exact number or an estimate.
  - A time frame or date when you would like to receive this information.

In some instances, this set of questions can be incorporated within the needs assessment (discussed in Chapter 6).

Describe Relevant Characteristics of Program Participants

You can accomplish the task of describing relevant characteristics of those who will participate in a sport psychology program through one of the three methods already discussed above. For this task the key question is:

What characteristics of the program participants—based on what you know about them—can guide subsequent steps in the program development process, particularly needs assessment and context assessment?

In order to specify characteristics of participants for a sport psychology program, it may be relevant to obtain and describe particular information about the participants. The following framework suggests various characteristics you may want to identify:

- *Demographic Characteristics*
  - Age of the athletes
  - Gender
  - Number of years of experience playing the sport
- *Socio-Cultural Characteristics*
  - Values and personal expectations toward sport and life
  - Linguistic proficiency
  - Family constellation
- *Educational Characteristics*
  - Level of academic achievement
  - Academic major
  - Participation in continued education courses or activities.

The task of describing program participants' characteristics will result in information that can help you to decide how to develop the needs assessment and context assessment.

Table 5.1 reflects relevant characteristics of participants in a mental performance program that I designed and implemented with members of a National Basketball Association (NBA) team.

Determine Segmentation of Program Participants

Segmentation of program participants involves dividing the larger group of athletes into more specific stratifications. Segmentation typically occurs based on the descriptive information that you already have obtained on the relevant characteristics of the program participants.

The segmentation of program participants is especially important when there are likely to be large numbers of participants spread across a range

Table 5.1 Relevant characteristics of participants for a mental performance program (NBA team)

Demographics	*Number of participants*	12
	Chronological age range of participants	19.2–37.1
	Years of experience playing professional basketball	
	0–1	3
	2–5	4
	6–10	3
	11+	2
Socio-cultural characteristics	*Priority personal expectations*	
	Be a consistent performer	4
	Balance basketball and life	2
	Be a good teammate/contributor	2
	Earn a good living	4
	Dominant/Native language	
	English	8
	Spanish	2
	Russian	1
	Italian	1
	Family status	
	Married	7
	Not married	5
	Children (overall)	14
Educational characteristics	*Education*	
	College graduate	4
	1–3 years of college	7
	High school graduate	12

of competitive levels, organizations, and program sites. Accordingly, here are segments that may be relevant to consider as you assess segmentation, depending on the nature and scope of the program:

- School
- Grade level
- Team
- Position on team
- Other.

Professional Practice Exercises

1. Think about athletes who have participated in sport psychology programs that you have designed or observed being designed. What were the most important characteristics of these athletes? Was there any other information that you would have liked to obtain about them so that they could have been characterized in a more specific way for program development purposes?

2. How can you make the case to a client, such as a coach or athletic administrator, that specifying the target population for a program is an important step that should not be overlooked?

6
ASSESSING THE NEEDS OF PROGRAM PARTICIPANTS

The purpose of this chapter is to provide guidelines about how to formulate and conduct a needs assessment of the athletes or others who will be participating in a sport psychology program. Needs assessment is essential so that the resultant information can be used as a basis for designing the program. First, this chapter offers a rationale for needs assessment and a definition of a sport psychology program "need." Second, it describes a list of qualities for an appropriate needs assessment. Third, it covers how to formulate a needs assessment that focuses on learning about the mental and emotional needs of program participants.

Rationale for a Sport Psychology Program Needs Assessment

If a sport psychology program is going to have value for its participants, then it is vital to conduct an assessment of the mental and emotional needs of the participants (Maher, 2012). A needs assessment, coupled with assessment of the relevant organizational context in which the program will be embedded (covered in Chapter 7), offers a baseline for designing a sport psychology program. Without needs assessment information to guide the design of a program, you can shortchange the entire sport psychology program development process. Failure to assess important mental and emotional needs of program participants will result in limitations of the program's ability to meet needs, since needs will be unknown.

However, when a sport psychology program needs assessment is formulated and conducted in an appropriate manner, the resultant needs assessment information will lead to a more informed design of a sport psychology program (AERA, APA, & NCME, 2014).

Definition of a Sport Psychology Program Need

A "sport psychology program need" represents the gap between a current situation and a desired situation of program participants in relation to their performance or personal development. More specifically, the gap—the need—reflects knowledge, skills, or abilities that program participants, such as athletes, need to develop in order to be the best versions of themselves as performers and people (Maher, 2011). These identified gaps can be labeled as the mental and emotional needs of program participants (Maher, 2012).

A sport psychology program needs assessment is the process used to gather information about these gaps so that a program can be designed and implemented in relation to one or more needs (Kaufman, 2000; Maher, 2012). In other words, the needs assessment information you obtain will inform you, your client, and others about what program participants need to develop, improve, or strengthen with regard to particular knowledge, skills, or abilities. This kind of information will assist you in making decisions about how to design a sport psychology program that addresses one or more of the identified needs.

For example, you may determine through a needs assessment that the members of a college baseball team could benefit from improving their mental discipline prior to games though the use of effective routines. This is a statement of "need," because it recognizes and highlights the important gap that exists between the current and desired situations:

> *Current Situation* – Players on the team are inconsistent with their mental discipline prior to games.
> *Desired Situation* – Players on the team are consistently mentally disciplined prior to games.

Here is another example of a sport psychology need that was based on a needs assessment:

> *Current Situation* – Members of a professional ice hockey team lack the capacity to cope effectively with less than desirable game performances.

Desired Situation – Members of a professional ice hockey team are able to cope in an effective way with less than desirable game performances.

It is important to note here that this definition of need—as a gap between a current situation and a more desired situation—is very specific and intentional. I have used this definition of need to call attention to what athletes need to improve or move toward with regard to their mental and emotional development.

This definition of need, though, stands in contrast to how the term "need" has been used in sport psychology. For example, it sometimes is said that athletes "need" a program, such as a mental skills program, or that they "need" sport psychology assistance. Yet with regard to the program development process that we are covering in this book, the program is not the need. Rather, the program is a solution or response to one or more needs. Thus, the design of the program (solution) should be based on the needs of those who will be participating in the program. In terms of program development, the following principle applies: Needs of program participants drive programs; programs are solutions, not the needs.

Therefore, a needs assessment reflects two situations with regard to program participants:

1. *Current Situation* – This is the situation where needs assessment information indicates that the athletes (program participants) do not possess particular levels of knowledge, skills, or abilities that if possessed would make them a better performer or person.
2. *Desired Situation* – This is the anticipated future situation wherein athletes possess particular knowledge, skills, or abilities that make them a better performer or person.

Figure 6.1 is a visual illustration of the notion of sport psychology need as a gap between a current situation and a desired situation with respect to those athletes or others for whom a program is going to be designed and implemented.

The gap between the current situation and the desired situation, as illustrated in Figure 6.1, is the sport psychology program need. In turn, the program you design serves as the means or solution to address the need—that

Figure 6.1 Sport psychology need.

is, it will close the gap between the current situation and the desired situation. (Program design will be covered in Chapter 8.)

A sport psychology program that is designed based on needs assessment information as well as context assessment information (covered in Chapter 7) increases the likelihood that the program will add value to program participants. It also makes the program more likely to be able to sustain itself following implementation and over the course of time in the organization.

Qualities of an Appropriate Needs Assessment

The process of a needs assessment for a sport psychology program, therefore, includes gathering and using needs assessment information as a basis to inform you and others about how to design a successful program. This process relies on defining sport psychology need as the gap between a current situation and a desired situation with regard to particular knowledge, skills, or abilities of those athletes or others who will participate in the future program.

In my work designing, implementing, and evaluating sport psychology programs in professional and collegiate settings, I have found needs assessment to be crucial to the process and tasks of program development. This has been the case no matter how large or small the program. The five qualities necessary for an appropriate needs assessment for sport psychology program development to occur are the following:

1. *Professional Competence* – The individual who is responsible for formulating and conducting the needs assessment must have the education and training to engage in the assessment task in accordance

with the ethical standards of the Association of Applied Sport Psychology and the standards of the American Psychological Association. More specifically, this individual has to understand the process of program development; they must be competent in the use of data collection methods and instruments and must be adept at the formulation of customized rating scales and forms (AERA et al., 2014).

2. *Practicality* – The needs assessment should be capable of being implemented in a practical manner. More important, the needs assessment should not disrupt operating routines of the organization in which it will occur.

3. *Utility* – The needs assessment should result in information that serves two purposes: (a) assists in deciding how to proceed with the design of a program in light of the needs of program participants; and (b) identifies particular mental and emotional needs of program participants that may be addressed through a sport psychology program.

4. *Propriety* – The needs assessment must be conducted adhering to relevant ethical codes, rules, and regulations for data collection, such as those embodied in the codes of ethics of the American Psychological Association and the Association for Advancement of Sport Psychology.

5. *Technical Defensibility* – The needs assessment involves the use of methods, procedures, and instruments that you can justify as content-valid and otherwise appropriate, given the information you are seeking (AERA et al., 2014).

Needs Assessment Guidelines

Needs assessment is the process of gathering information about the current situation and desired situation gaps of program participants. The discrepancy reflects the gap between a current situation and a more desired situation with regard to the knowledge, skills, or abilities of those who will be participating in a sport psychology program.

The following are guidelines for formulating and conducting an appropriate needs assessment to use as a basis for sport psychology program development:

- Identify the program participants.
- Delineate needs assessment questions.
- Select data collection methods and procedures.
- Construct a needs assessment protocol.
- Implement the protocol.

Identify the Program Participants

A needs assessment is intended to capture information about the needs of particular program participants (e.g., athletes) for whom a decision will be made about whether and to what extent a sport psychology program may be warranted. Typically, the program participants for a needs assessment will be athletes. However, the participants for a sport psychology program may be another group, such as coaches, parents of athletes, or educational administrators.

Whatever the case, you must specify the individuals who will participate in the program, since the program that will be developed is intended for them and not for another group. The task of how to specify the participants for a sport psychology program has already been covered in Chapter 5.

Delineate Needs Assessment Questions

A clearly stated needs assessment question reveals how you will obtain relevant and available information about the program participants. A needs assessment question addresses the program participants and thus should not be confused with questions on surveys or questionnaires that interested parties may complete.

Following are actual examples from my professional practice of needs assessment questions for various types of program participants. Keeping in mind what we mean by "need" (as discussed earlier in this chapter), you should find that the answers to these questions allow you to become more informed about the current situation. This can help you then delineate a more desired situation and, thus, identify needs.

Athletes

- To what extent do athletes need to become more effective at balancing their sport with the rest of their lives?
- Do the athletes possess necessary skills that will prepare them to be mentally and emotionally ready to compete?

- How knowledgeable are the athletes regarding how to cope effect-ively with poor performance and adverse situations?
- What skills do the athletes need to improve or acquire so they will be able to pay attention to what matters in the competitive moment?
- To what degree are the athletes accurate evaluators of their performance?

Coaches

- In what ways do coaches possess skills that will allow them to be effective communicators with their athletes?
- To what extent do coaches need to learn about athlete mental health?
- What skills do coaches need to learn so they can be effective at man-aging individual and team conflict?

Parents

- What do parents of athletes need to learn about sport psychology?
- What parenting skills will help them in their interaction with their children and the coaches of their children?

Select Data Collection Methods and Procedures

There are several ways that you can collect information in order to answer needs assessment questions such as the questions provided above. These methods are:

- Focus Group Method
- Survey Method
- Discussion Method.

Focus Group Method

In this method, individuals meet as a group and discuss their responses to one or more needs assessment questions. As potential participants in a program, these individuals should be familiar with the sport and its demands on them.

For example, with regard to the task of developing a program for athletes, members of a focus group may include:

- All or some of the athletes for whom a sport psychology program is being considered.

- The coaches and the support staff for athletes who know the athletes and have had contact with them.
- Parents of the athletes.
- Outside experts such as sport psychologists and mental skills coaches who are familiar with the sport and its demands.

The opinions and perspectives shared in the needs assessment focus group should give you data for your needs assessment.

Survey Method

A needs assessment survey instrument consists of a written set of items (questions or statements) that are intended to elicit responses from those completing the instrument. Accordingly, the survey items should be guided by particular needs assessment questions. For example, the following survey has provided useful information about needs of athletes. It is based on the needs assessment question, "What are areas of mental and emotional development in which athletes need to become more proficient?"

EXAMPLE OF A NEEDS ASSESSMENT SURVEY INSTRUMENT: ATHLETES

(CAN BE COMPLETED BY ATHLETES ABOUT THEMSELVES OR BY COACHES ABOUT THEIR ATHLETES)

Rate each item using the following scale: 3 = possesses consistent skill in this area; 2 = fair but need to improve in this area; 1 = much need to develop skill in this area

> ____ 1. *Perspective* – balances sport effectively with the rest of life.
> ____ 2. *Personal Awareness* – accurately evaluates strong points and limitations.
> ____ 3. *Self-Motivation* – sets goals that are specific, measurable, and energizing.
> ____ 4. *Mental Discipline* – follows through on performance plans and routines.
> ____ 5. *Self-Confidence* – believes in the capacity to execute during competition.
> ____ 6. *Emotional Intensity* – competes at an effective level of energy and effort.

_____ 7. *Focus* – pays attention to what matters in the moment during competition.

_____ 8. *Composure* – remains poised under competitive pressure.

_____ 9. *Teamwork* – interacts productively with coaches and others.

_____10. *Self-Esteem* – separates oneself as a person from oneself as a performer.

_____11. *Performance Accountability* – manifests responsibility for one's results.

_____12. *Continuous Improvement* – strives to grow and develop, despite obstacles.

If the participants for a program are a group of coaches, and if the intent is to consider the design of a coach mental education program for them, you may want to use something like the following example survey instrument. It is based on the needs assessment question, "What would you like to become more knowledgeable about or skilled in so that you can be a better coach with regard to the mental side of sport?"

EXAMPLE OF A NEEDS ASSESSMENT SURVEY INSTRUMENT: COACHES

Please check the three (3) areas that you would like to learn more about and become skilled in:

_____ 1. Balancing my role as a coach with the rest of my life.

_____ 2. Developing effective coaching routines.

_____ 3. Managing and resolving conflict with difficult athletes.

_____ 4. Communicating with other coaches.

_____ 5. Identifying indicators of athlete stress.

_____ 6. How and when to refer athletes with suspected mental health problems.

_____ 7. Other (please describe) _____.

Discussion Method

This method of needs assessment is the most informal method. It is best to use when neither a focus group or survey instrument is practical or possible. This method involves meeting with those individuals who have good familiarity with the mental and emotional needs of program participants, especially if they are athletes. You should discuss with them the following:

- What they consider to be the mental and emotional development needs important to address for program participants at this time.
- What mental skills will make the athletes better performers at this time.
- What areas of team development are important to consider.

Construct a Needs Assessment Protocol

A needs assessment protocol is the roadmap for conducting the needs assessment. It is based on having completed prior steps as described above. In essence, a needs assessment protocol includes information about the following areas:

- *Program Participants* – A clear description of the participants for whom a sport psychology program is being considered and on whom the needs assessment will be conducted.
- *Needs Assessment Questions* – The specific questions that will drive the collection of needs assessment data to answer the questions.
- *Data Collection Methods and Procedures* – How the data about the needs of program participants will be obtained, such as by means of a focus group, survey, or discussion with relevant stakeholders. This entails ascertaining whether informed consent and confidentiality is part of the needs assessment process.
- *Roles and Responsibilities* – Who will be involved in data collection and how they will make sure that the data are collected in an appropriate manner.
- *Timelines and Location* – When and where needs assessment activities will occur.
- *Use of Needs Assessment Information* – Who will have access to needs assessment results and who will make sure that the information is provided in an appropriate form.

Implement the Needs Assessment Protocol

A written needs assessment protocol that addresses the elements listed above will now be ready for implementation. Once you have received approval to proceed, your task then is to follow through with a commitment to the protocol, implementing the assessment as planned, making adjustments in it as you proceed.

Table 6.1 Example of a needs assessment protocol

Program participants	25 members of a 40-man roster MLB team
Needs assessment questions	Given your role on the team, what are the challenges that you face that you would like to get better at handling? What would you like to learn more about with regard to the mental side of the game?
Data collection methods and procedures	Focus group of all position players Focus group of all pitchers Mental skills checklist (Maher, 2011) One-on-one meeting with all players
Roles and responsibilities	Team sport psychologist and the mental performance coach will conduct the need assessment. Due to the Collective Bargaining Agreement of Major League Baseball, participation in the need assessment is voluntary. Participants will complete informed consent forms.
Timeline and location	Data collection will occur between February 10 and 15. Team's spring training Development Complex
Use of needs assessment information	Needs assessment results to be used by team sport psychologist as a basis for designing and implementing mental skills programs for spring training and the season.

Table 6.1 is an example of a needs assessment protocol, using the above framework.

Professional Practice Exercises

1. What experiences have you had conducting needs assessments as a basis for developing a sport psychology program? What went well with this kind of needs assessment? How could you improve the needs assessment process?

2. Consider the professionals with whom you work or consult with regard to making decisions about when and how to develop sport psychology programs. How could you propose to them how to proceed to conduct an appropriate needs assessment?

7

DETERMINING RELEVANT ORGANIZATIONAL CONTEXT

The purpose of this chapter is to provide guidelines for determining the relevant organizational context in which the needs of the program participants, such as athletes, are embedded. First, the chapter offers a rationale for determining the relevant organizational context. Second, it describes a practical, proven framework for organizational context assessment. Third, it covers methods and procedures for conducting an organizational context assessment and addresses what to do with the information you obtain.

Rationale for Determining Relevant Organizational Context

Sport psychology programs are implemented in organizations (Fletcher & Wagstaff, 2009). These organizations may be sports organizations, such as a professional sports franchise, or they may be part of educational institutions, such as a department of intercollegiate athletics. Without doubt, the organization and its context are important considerations for the design and implementation of sport psychology programs. Consequently, determining relevant aspects of the organizational context is essential for developing and sustaining sport psychology programs.

The task of determining the relevant context of the organization in which a sport psychology program will be designed and implemented is necessary for one very basic reason: a sport psychology program does not exist in a vacuum or a research laboratory. Rather, such a program occurs in real time, with a range of people, places, and circumstances.

Clearly, organizational context has to be taken into account in terms of program design and implementation. Accordingly, you cannot relegate organizational context to laboratory control or error variance. You instead must consider it an essential aspect of the sport psychology program development process.

Definition of Relevant Organizational Context

With regard to the sport psychology program development process, "relevant organizational context" refers to the social, cultural, systemic, political, and other factors that comprise the organization (Clauss-Ehlers, Chiriboga, Hunter, Roysircar, & Tummala-Narra, 2019). You should take these factors into account when deciding whether and to what extent a sport psychology program should be developed for program participants, whether the participants are athletes, coaches, support staff, or administrators.

More basically, organizational factors can influence which mental and emotional needs of the program participants the program can reasonably address. Thus, these factors are relevant for designing a program, implementing it, and deciding if the program should and can be sustained over the course of time.

An organizational context assessment is the means for determining relevant organizational context. This kind of assessment involves obtaining information about what is relevant concerning the context in which a sport psychology program may be designed and in which it will be implemented. In this regard, I have found that an organizational context assessment, appropriately conducted, will inform you and your client about whether and to what extent a sport psychology program should be designed and implemented, if at all. Without such a context assessment, any sport psychology program will be developed—literally—out of context, thereby increasing the likelihood that it will not be valuable or sustainable.

Framework for an Organizational Context Assessment

An organizational context assessment should be conducted once you have assessed the mental and emotional needs of program participants (covered in Chapter 6). This kind of context assessment, therefore, should be considered as integral to the Clarification Phase of the sport psychology program development process.

Ability

Values

Ideas

Circumstances

Timing

Obligation

Resistance

Yield

Figure 7.1 AVICTORY framework.

The following framework will help as you conduct an organizational context assessment. I find the framework to be indispensable in my work with developing sport psychology programs. It will allow you to determine which factors of the organizational context to assess and how to obtain information about those factors. I refer to that framework as the AVICTORY framework. Using the acronym as your framework will help greatly in formulating and conducting an organizational context assessment.

Nature and Scope of the AVICTORY framework

The AVICTORY framework comprises eight contextual factors (see Figure 7.1). These are factors likely to influence the extent to which an organization is ready for a sport psychology program. Your knowledge of them will help guide you when designing and implementing such a program.

These eight factors are:

1. A: *Ability* – This refers to the extent to which an organization is able to commit resources to develop a sport psychology program. These resources include program staff and other personnel, information, facilities, location, time, and monetary funds.
2. V: *Values* – This factor evaluates the norms and traditions—cultural, social, political—in the organization that reveal what coaches, support staff, and administrators say and otherwise manifest about developing the total athlete, mentally and emotionally.
3. I: *Ideas* – This organizational factor considers what people who are part of the organization, including coaches, support staff, and athletic administrators, think about sport psychology.
4. C: *Circumstances* – This factor reflects the stability of the organization in terms of leadership and personnel; it considers the staying power of those who will champion and otherwise support a sport psychology program.
5. T: *Timing* – This factor addresses the extent to which the current time of year or season is opportune for sport psychology program design and implementation.
6. O: *Obligation* – This is the degree to which key stakeholders and others in the organization feel obliged and otherwise committed to sport psychology in the organization.
7. R: *Resistance* – This factor refers to those in the organization who may resist efforts to build a sport psychology program.
8. Y: *Yield* – This factor concerns the perceived benefits of a sport psychology program as expressed by athletes, coaches, and other stakeholders.

Methods and Procedures for Obtaining Information about Organizational Context Factors

In your role as practitioner, there are various ways to obtain information about these eight factors for an organizational context assessment. Your role in the program development process, your knowledge of the organization, and your relationship with your client and others, including athletes and coaches, will determine how you acquire the information.

In the following, I have listed the methods and procedures that I have found to be practical and effective in obtaining information on the eight factors. These methods and procedures are:

- Discussions with your client about all of the eight factors.
- Focus groups with athletes about the Values, Ideas, and Yield factors.
- Individual or small group meetings with coaches about the Ideas, Values, and Obligation factors.
- Meetings with athletic administrators to discuss the Ability, Circumstances, Timing, and Resistance factors.
- Review of documents about the organization and its context with attention to all eight factors.
- Observations of the operations of the athletic department or team with respect to the Values, Ideas, Obligation, and Resistance factors.
- Brief surveys of athletes with regard to the Ideas and Yield factors.

In addition to these examples of methods and procedures for obtaining information about the eight organizational context factors, the following paragraphs provide a more detailed description of what information to seek with regard to each organizational factor.

Ability to Commit Resources

In order for a sport psychology program to be designed, implemented, and sustained, the organization in which the program will occur needs to commit resources. The extent to which resources are available in the organization will determine whether the program can be designed and implemented.

In order to develop a sport psychology program that will have value to program participants and other relevant stakeholders, most of these organizational resources will need to be available:

- *Human Resources* – These resources are the individuals who need to be employed or available and who are necessary for a program to occur. Human resources include people such as the implementers of the program, consultants necessary to support program design and implementation, those funding the program, and, of course, available athletes or other target populations for whom the program is going to be provided.
- *Technological Resources* – These resources are those that allow the program to operate effectively in relation to its participants. Depending on the nature and scope of the program, technological resources may include computers, biofeedback equipment, notebooks, journals, and other kinds of material products. Specific psychological

and educational methods, protocols, and procedures that will be used as part of the program to obtain program goals are also considered technological resources.

- *Informational Resources* – These resources comprise the information necessary to assist in the design and implementation of the program and, thus, to provide direction for the program. Informational resources include the description of the size and scope of the program's target population, the needs assessment results, and program goals. Criteria for eligibility into the program, policies and procedures that guide program operation, and any other useful information pertaining to the program also fall into this category.
- *Physical Resources* – Physical resources are tangible products or spaces in which the program will be implemented. They include offices, player meeting rooms, courts and playing fields, and other physical features where the program will be held.
- *Financial Resources* – Financial resources are the monetary funds necessary for a program to be designed and implemented. These may include funds for staff and consultant salaries, field and room rentals, and liability insurance. Without an appropriate amount of money budgeted for a sport psychology program, there is little possibility that the program will come to fruition in any meaningful way.

Values within the Organization

Values reflect the statements, norms, and traditions that are expressed by people in the organization. This is especially the case for those, such as executives and coaches, who influence how psychology programs and services are introduced and operate in the organization. In particular, it is important for you to learn how coaches, athletic administrators, and front office executives value both the mental side of sport and the investment of time and funds in this area. If they do not consider the mental side of sport a high priority, then you will not be surprised if they devalue a sport psychology program or view it as tangential to the operations of the organization.

In addition, as you address the values organizational factor, you will find it helpful to learn the organization's history of assisting athletes with their mental and emotional development, not only as performers but also as people outside competitive venues. In this regard, a key, overarching question asks whether organizational members have judged sport psychology and related services as a waste of time, as superfluous activities, or as important to the development of their athletes.

Furthermore, it is useful to learn how coaches and others consider the cultural diversity and ethnicity of athletes and staff. Another important question is: Do organizational members believe that athletes are a select group and therefore entitled to sport psychology programs, or do they believe that these types of programs are necessary for athlete development?

Ideas about Sport Psychology

This organizational factor considers what people who are part of the organization think about sport psychology—what it is and what it is not. In essence, it evaluates what ideas athletes, coaches, and athletic administrators, including your client, envisage when you talk about a sport psychology program. For example, there are likely to be instances where individuals think of a sport psychology program as a "magic bullet," something that will turbo charge the performance of athletes. Others may believe that a sport psychology program is designed to make sure that athletes possess some psychological quality. In other instances, some members of the organization will have no idea whatsoever about what is meant by a sport psychology program.

Understanding the ideas that people have about sport psychology and sport psychology programs can assist you in deciding what kinds of education or discussions may be needed as part of the program development process. In turn, this kind of information can help you determine whether and to what extent you can design a sport psychology program that will have value for its participants.

Circumstances within the Organization

The factor of organizational circumstances evaluates the stability of the organization with regard to its leadership structure and overall stability. For example, if the director of a college division of intercollegiate athletics who is an advocate of sport psychology and sport psychology programs will be departing from that post at the end of the year, then it may not be clear, circumstantially, as to whether the next director will take the same stance regarding those matters. This lack of certainty may lead you to suggest delaying the start of a program until the next director comes aboard and you are able to learn their views.

In contrast, consider the example of a highly successful head coach of a professional football team who has been supportive of sport psychology and who just has been awarded a multi-year contract extension. You likely will decide that this scenario offers more stable circumstances than the other example, leading you to move forward with the development of a sport psychology program or the refinement of an existing one.

Timing of a Program

In an organizational context, timing may very well be everything, as the saying goes. One of the realities of program planning work that I often encounter is the need to ascertain whether the timing is right to initiate the development of a program. Here are examples of organizational situations, or scenarios, which relate to timing and that I have encountered in my work where I have had to consider questions of timing:

- It is the end of the spring semester, and those who need to be involved in developing a sport psychology program are leaving for the summer and vacations.
- The new athletic director wants to begin to develop a sport psychology program for student-athletes and wants to initiate program development efforts immediately.
- The head women's lacrosse coach has expressed interest in developing a sport psychology program for her team, but she wants to wait until the summer before deciding how to proceed.
- The state legislature just authorized funds in the new state budget that will release substantial money to address the mental health needs of athletes and coaches in public high schools, colleges, and universities in the state.

Obligation for a Program

The development of a sport psychology program involves considerable work, effort, and support on the part of many people. After all, among other tasks, development includes needs assessment, program design, and successful implementation of the program.

In my experiences, I have found that sport psychology program development will proceed more smoothly with the assistance of one to two other people who also feel obligated to develop a successful program. Without others who share a sense of obligation, your ability to develop a program that has value for a target population may very well be limited in nature and scope.

When you identify those who have expressed such an obligation, do what you can to thank them and to express your willingness to communicate and collaborate with them.

Examples of obligated organizational members are likely to be:

- You, in your role as practitioner.
- Your client.
- The executive or director who oversees sport operations.
- A particular member of the athletic staff.
- A mental performance coach.
- Athletes who are likely to participate in the program.

Resistance to a Program

While there may be some people who are obligated to work to ensure the development of a sport psychology program, there also may be individuals and groups within the organization who will resist program development efforts and hinder the successful implementation of a program. Your task here—to identify those who may resist and assess the nature and scope of the resistance—may not be that easy, since some of the resistance may be covert or passive.

Individuals and groups who may manifest forms of program resistance include the following examples:

- Coaches who may be asked to help develop or participate in a program.
- Athletes who currently may be taxed due to their schedules and amount of daily work.
- Officials of the unions that represent players in professional sports.
- Others.

Examples of behaviors that signify resistance in the organization are:

- Failure to attend meetings about the program.
- Refusal to complete forms or mental skills checklists.

- Publication or sharing of memos or news articles that predict problems if the program happens/succeeds.
- Vocal statements about why a program is not necessary or warranted.

If such resistance is identified, then you can determine how you may want to deal with it, either formally through meetings or informally by means of discussions with appropriate parties.

Yield from a Program

Yield involves positive and/or negative perceptions by those in the organization about the results arising from the program's implementation in their organization. Examples of the perceptions of yield, or benefit, are:

- The athletes will become stronger mentally and emotionally.
- The athletic department will be viewed as standing on the cutting edge of mental performance.
- Those who fund the programs and services that support athletes will feel that their dollars are being spent in a productive way.
- The program will be a waste of time, effort, and money.
- The program is only occurring to give the general manager a feather in their cap.

What to do with Organizational Context Information

You can use the organizational context information that you gather in your role as a practitioner to answer the following questions:

1. *Ability* – To what extent are resources—human, technological, information, physical, financial—available and sufficient to begin the task of designing a sport psychology program for a target population in conjunction with needs assessment results?
2. *Values* – Are the norms and traditions in the organization conducive to the development of the total athlete and, in particular, to their mental and emotional development?
3. *Ideas* – What do ideas of sport psychology and sport psychology programs mean to athletes, coaches, and administrators who will receive or otherwise be involved in a program?

4. *Circumstances* – How stable is the organization in terms of leadership and structure?
5. *Timing* – To what extent is the current time an appropriate time to initiate the development of a sport psychology program?
6. *Obligation* – Who are the people obligated to collaborate with me to ensure that a sport psychology program is designed and implemented in a way that will have value for all those involved?
7. *Resistance* – Who are the individuals and groups who may offer resistance to the program?
8. *Yield* – What do athletes, coaches, and others perceive to be the benefits of the program, and for whom are these benefits?

Professional Practice Exercises

1. In your professional experiences, what factors have constrained the development of sport psychology programs? What factors facilitated their design and implementation?
2. How have you dealt with resistance to sport psychology programs in organizations in which you have been employed or provided services as an external consultant?

PART III
DESIGN PHASE

Establishing the Purpose and Goals of the Program
Organizing the Program Design
Putting the Program Design into an Evaluable Form

Clarification   Design   Implementation   Evaluation

8

ESTABLISHING THE PURPOSE AND GOALS OF THE PROGRAM

This chapter provides guidelines for establishing the purpose of a sport psychology program as well as guidelines for setting program goals. The chapter offers a rationale for establishing a program purpose and set of program goals. Then it describes the parameters of a statement of program purpose (including its three basic elements), provides examples, and explains the construction of a statement of program purpose. Next, we turn attention to program goals: how to determine goals that are appropriate for the program and how to place them into a SMART form.

An important first step of the Design Phase of the sport psychology program development process includes the task of achieving clarity regarding the purpose of the sport psychology program to which program goals are linked. The purpose and goals of a sport psychology program, no matter how large or small in nature and scope the program may be, are basic reference points for determining how to organize the design of the program. They help you to place the program in a form so that it can be evaluated following implementation.

Rationale for a Statement of Program Purpose and Program Goals

During my many years of professional practice in sport and performance psychology, I have become convinced of the following: certain conditions are essential in order for you to design and implement a sport psychology program that adds value to its participants as well as to the organization in which the program is embedded. First, you need clear and documented evidence of the purpose of the program, that is, its overall reason for being. Second, you must have goals for the program participants that, if attained, will make these participants better as performers or people (Locke & Latham, 2002). Third, you must base the statement of program purpose and program goals on the characteristics of program participants, their needs assessment results, and relevant organizational context, disclosed during the Clarification Phase (covered in Chapters 5, 6, and 7).

If these essential conditions are met, then it will be clear to you, your client, and others how a sport psychology program can be designed for those participants for whom the program is intended within the relevant context of the organization. In contrast, without such benchmarks—that is, without purpose and goals linked to needs of program participants—your ability to design the program, implement it, and make judgments about its value will be limited or, more likely, random at best.

Definition of a Statement of Program Purpose

A statement of purpose of a sport psychology program is a way of summarizing important elements of the program before it begins. In this regard, a statement of program purpose will be beneficial to your clients and others in the following ways:

- The statement of program purpose will inform your client and others about who will receive the program, how it will be implemented, and what it is intended to accomplish. This is a necessary starting point for the organization of the design of the program (to be covered in Chapter 9).
- The program purpose statement will serve as a default position, if and when a program goes off course in terms of its implementation. It has the power to refocus everyone back to its reason for being.
- The statement allows you to link clearly the program's goals to its purpose.
- It is a reference point when engaging in program evaluation.

It is very important to note here that a statement of program purpose relates to the program and not to individual goals of the athlete (which may be part of an athlete's individual plan or an individual intervention for an athlete). Also, although it might seem that a statement of program purpose is similar to the notion of a mission statement often used in business settings, it is different because the program purpose statement is concerned with only one program in one context. In addition, it is based on information that has been generated as part of the Clarification Phase.

Three Elements of a Statement of Program Purpose

A statement of purpose for a sport psychology program will be meaningful for the organization of the design of the program if the statement is formulated in relation to three elements: Who, How, and What.

WHO – This element refers to the participants of the program, that is, those athletes or others who are expected to be involved in the program and for whom it is being designed. Granted, at this point in the process, it may not be possible to know all of the participants in the program. Nevertheless, the WHO element draws attention to the fact that without a clearly defined target population for the program, it will be difficult, if not impossible, to design the program in any meaningful or customized manner.

HOW – This element focuses attention on the program's organization in terms of aspects such as its components or phases as well as the methods, procedures, and activities that will constitute the core of the program. Here, too, you may not be clear yet about all of the methods or procedures you will use in the program. However, at a minimum, the HOW element of a program purpose statement places emphasis on how the program is likely to be organized so that it can be implemented successfully, according to program design.

WHAT – This third element relates to the anticipated value of the program for its participants. By value, I am referring to the knowledge, skills, or abilities that the athletes or others gain through their participation in the program. Typically, the goals of the program reflect the knowledge, skills, and abilities that program participants accrue.

Examples of Statements of Program Purpose

Keeping in mind the three essential elements of a statement of program purpose as described above, I offer some examples of statements of purpose of several sport psychology programs that I have designed and implemented. These examples have been selected randomly from my files and, as such,

I have not used the names of program participants and the teams and settings where the programs occurred in order to protect confidentiality.

These examples are:

Mental Skills Development Program for Minor League Baseball Players

WHO – Minor league players in the organization's player development system who have two years or less of professional baseball service, including pitchers and position players alike.

HOW – Through didactic presentations and small group skill building, which mental skills coaches will conduct over the course of the fall development period, players will be provided a program to assist them in the development of several mental skills: Perspective, Mental Discipline, Confidence, Focus, Accurate Self-Evaluation.

WHAT – As a result of their participation in the program, the players will learn (1) how to become consistent in preparing to compete; (2) how to maintain productive mind in the moment presence; and (3) how to deal accurately and productively with the results of their performances.

Team Development Program for an NBA Team

WHO – Players who are on the roster of the NBA team for the current season.

HOW – Players will participate in weekly team meetings, with the facilitation of the sport psychologist and head coach, that will teach them how to cope in an effective way with things they as a team can control.

WHAT – As a result of their participation in this program, players will learn to formulate and implement a team mutual accountability process and follow through on it so that they can work together as a team before, during, and after games.

Individual Mental Performance Plan System for College Student-Athletes

WHO – Student-athletes of the men's and women's basketball teams of a Division I collegiate athletic department.

HOW – Student-athletes will be involved with their coaches and the sport psychologist in the design and implementation of individual mental performance plans. These plans will be based on an individual mental skills assessment and will include mental goals, planned activities, and progress evaluation criteria.

WHAT – Through the collaboration with their coaches and the sport psychologist, we anticipate that the student-athletes will make progress toward attaining their mental goals.

How to Construct a Statement of Purpose for a Sport Psychology Program

If you have completed the Clarification Phase of the program development process (covered in Chapters 5, 6, and 7), you will have the information you need to construct a statement of program purpose. This clarification information includes the specification of program participants, their mental and emotional needs related to their sport, and the relevant organization in which the sport psychology program will be embedded.

Here is how to proceed in the task of constructing a statement of sport psychology program purpose:

1. Begin by making sure that you have specified the participants for which the program is going to be designed. This includes making sure that you have information on their mental and emotional needs that the program will address and information on the context in which the program will occur. (If you do not have program participant needs assessment information and/or context assessment information, it will be difficult to establish a meaningful statement of purpose. Therefore, my advice is to obtain such information before you proceed with designing the program.)

2. Assuming that you have information on program participants, their mental and emotional needs, and the relevant organizational context, take the first element, WHO, and provide an overview statement about the anticipated participants in the program.

3. Next, take the second element, HOW, and begin to consider the manner in which you will organize the program. This includes thinking about the methods, procedures, and activities that you will likely include as part of the program's design.

4. Then, take the third element, WHAT, and focus on the value that you expect the program to have for its participants. This consideration of program value will be helpful in setting program goals.

5. Finally, based on the information that you have produced for the WHO, HOW, and WHAT elements, write a draft of the statement of purpose for the program. At this point, consider this statement as a draft (a statement in progress). The examples that I provided in the prior section of this chapter may be helpful guides during this step.

6. When you establish the goals of the program and specify the manner in which the program is organized, you can return to the statement to revise it and place it in its final form.

Because your program purpose statement is tied to your program goals, the remaining sections of this chapter address the topic of program goals.

Definition of a Program Goal

A sport psychology program goal is a statement about how the participants will benefit from a program that is going to be designed for them. A program goal is not to be confused with an individual goal that an athlete may be pursuing (such as a goal that is part of an individual sport psychology intervention or individual mental plan). A program goal is derived from and linked to the statement of purpose of the program as well as from the information generated during the Clarification Phase (covered in Chapters 5, 6, and 7).

There are several reasons why program goals are important to the design, implementation, and evaluation of a sport psychology program. These reasons are:

- A sport psychology program goal guides you as you decide how to organize the program. In this regard, the program goal points to the kinds of methods and procedures that need to be incorporated into the program so that athletes or others will benefit from their participation in the program (Weinberg, 2010).
- A program goal can serve as a basis for evaluating the program once it has been implemented.
- A program goal signifies an important area of accomplishment or attainment by those athletes or others who are program participants.

Types of Program Goals

There are various types of program goals. In the broadest sense, any goal is a statement of intent. It signifies something that an individual, group, or organization will attain or accomplish. Goals are set in a range of areas of human functioning such as education, medicine, business, military, and sport. Regarding the area of sport psychology, we find individual goals and program goals. For the most part, individual goals and program goals are manifested by the acquisition or development of knowledge, skills, and abilities (that is, their KSAs).

Individual goals are set for one athlete, typically in relation to an individual mental plan or intervention for that individual. The focus for individual goals, therefore, centers on the individual and what they are striving to accomplish (McCarthy, 2019). An example of an individual goal for an athlete is:

> *For John to become consistent at maintaining a mind in the moment presence during competition.*

In contrast, *program goals* are established for a number or group of athletes: those who will be participating in a group program. A program goal thus concerns itself with an outcome—knowledge, skill, or ability—that it anticipates most, if not all, of a group of athletes will attain as they participate in the program organized and designed with them in mind. An example of a sport psychology program goal is:

> *For members of the women's lacrosse team to hold each other mutually accountable for how they prepare and compete, game to game.*

An *organizational goal* is a particular type of program goal that is connected to an organizational program, such as a department of sport psychology, and focuses on ensuring the organization operates in a productive manner. An organizational goal concerns itself with the processes that allow the organization to operate so that it has value to its athletes. An example of an organizational goal for a sports medicine department is:

> *For the sports medicine department to screen for the mental health needs of its student-athletes in a practical manner as part of its pre-participation protocol.*

As you think about your anticipated sport psychology program, you need to understand the type of goals that are being set and distinguish individual and organizational goals from program goals. These program goals will serve to dictate how the program is going to be organized with regard to methods, procedures, and activities (Maher, 2012).

Making Program Goals SMART

Since a program goal is a type of goal that is an integral part of the program development process, it should be made as SMART as possible. A SMART program goal will assist you in organizing the program and placing it into a program design that can be implemented and evaluated. A SMART program goal possesses the following properties:

- S: *Specific* – The goal is written in a specific enough way that program staff and others will know what knowledge, skill, or ability the program participants will acquire or develop.
- M: *Measurable* – The goal is structured so that there is an identifiable way to measure progress of the program's participants toward the goal.
- A: *Attainable* – Based on the information you have regarding the needs and context of program participants, your program goal assumes that all or most of them will be able to attain the goal.
- R: *Relevant* – Relevance reflects the belief that if the participant attains the goal, this success will contribute to the participant's mental and emotional development and performance.
- T: *Timing* – This refers to the expectation that program participants can attain the goal over a specified period of time, such as a season or semester.

Examples of Program Goals

I have been involved in the design of many sport psychology programs. Here are a few randomly selected examples from my files of some program goals I developed for various programs:

- Recently drafted players in the professional baseball organization will learn about growth mindsets and routines (taken from a minor league player foundations program).
- Member of the WNBA team will develop knowledge and skill so that they believe in their capacity to compete during game competition (taken from a mental skills development program).

- Athletic trainers will develop knowledge and understanding about players' mental skills (taken from a support staff continuing education program).
- The sport psychology department will provide a substance use education program for head and assistant coaches (taken from a sport psychology program service delivery program).
- Players will learn how to take responsibility for their competitive performance through the use of performance feedback (taken from a player performance improvement program).
- NBA coaches will learn how to assess and monitor themselves given their roles on the team (taken from a coach education program).

How to Establish Program Goals

Program goals are easy to discuss and to picture; however, it is not easy to establish and garner consensus on them. Here is a process that I found to be effective and efficient in establishing program goals—like those just listed in the examples above—for sport psychology programs:

1. Decide how many program goals you should set for your program. Although the size and scope of the program to be designed will determine and establish the actual number of goals, I have found that three or four program goals is a reasonable and realistically achievable number of goals for one program. If you are not sure as to whether there are a sufficient number of program goals or if there are too many, use the program's statement of purpose as the reference point for making that decision.

2. Make certain that you can justify each program goal based on the purpose of the program. More specifically, the statement of program purpose helps describes what the program is expected to accomplish. You should formulate your program goal with this expectation in mind. Accordingly, review the statement of purpose as well as the information you derived from the Clarification Phase, particularly needs assessment and context assessment information. Then, in order to keep your goals reasonable in number and in line with the program's purpose, decide if the goal under consideration is important enough to include as a program goal.

3. Construct a draft statement of the program goal that makes clear why you believe it merits inclusion in the program. As you do so, make

sure that the goal statement describes an outcome or accomplishment—knowledge, skill, or ability—for the program participants.

4. Once you have developed a program goal statement, try to make that goal as SMART as possible. You can review the program goal statement in relation to the following SMART program goal checklist (see Table 8.1), using the following rating scale of "Yes," "No," and "Not Sure."

- *Goal Specificity* – The goal is written in a way that is likely to be understood by those who will be involved with the program.
- *Goal Measurability* – The goal is specific enough that it will allow for one or more ways to determine the progress of the program's participants toward the goal.
- *Goal Attainability* – There is sufficient reason to believe that all or most of the participants will be able to attain the program goals.
- *Goal Relevance* – Research and experienced-based opinion support that their attainment of the goal will contribute to the mental and emotional development and performance of the participants.
- *Goal Time Frame* – Based on research and professional practice, the goal statement anticipates that most program participants will be able to attain the program goal over a prescribed period of time, such as during a semester or over the course of an entire season.

Table 8.1 SMART program goal checklist

	Yes	No	Not Sure
Specificity Measurability Attainability Relevance Time Frame			
Conclusion: □ Include goal in program goals □ More work needed □ Exclude goal			

5. Once you have considered each program goal in relation to this checklist, you will be able to make one of the following judgments about the program goal (see Table 8.1):

    • The program goal is SMART and thus should be included as part of the program (rated a "Yes" across all five of the above dimensions).

    • Work needs to occur on one or more of the dimensions of the SMART criteria (there were ratings of "No" or "Not Sure").

    • The program goal should not be included as part of the program due to any number of factors (e.g., it is too specific, or the resources are not available for the program to address the goal).

Professional Practice Exercises

1. Recall how you have set goals for sport psychology programs. Have the goals for these programs been centered on the knowledge, skills, and abilities of those who have participated in the program?

2. What do you believe are the typical obstacles to establishing the purpose and goals of a program? How can you overcome such obstacles in collaboration with others?

9
ORGANIZING THE PROGRAM DESIGN

The purpose of this chapter is to provide guidelines for an important program development task, one that often is overlooked or given cursory attention by those involved in developing sport psychology programs. The task involves organizing the design of the sport psychology program so that it can be implemented successfully and evaluated appropriately. First, I will cover the nature and scope of what it means to organize the design of the program. Second, I will provide steps you can take as you decide how to proceed in organizing the design of your program.

What It Means to Organize a Program

Over the years of my practice, I have observed many sport psychology programs that have been implemented successfully as well as programs that have not occurred as designed or have fizzled out. The difference between successfully implemented programs and less successful or failed programs correlates with program design: the successful ones have had a program design that was organized in a systematic and thoughtful manner.

I believe that any program, including any sport psychology program, is perfectly designed to get the results for which it was designed. In short, you get what you design. Accordingly, if the design of a sport psychology program is organized in a systematic and thoughtful manner, then chances increase that the program will be implemented as intended. Furthermore, the program is likely to be considered valuable and likely to continue to operate over the course of time (Maxwell, 2014). On the other hand, if the program's design is not organized well or is non-existent, it should not be surprising when the "program" fizzles out and/or when any of the program's results are less than expected (McEwan & Beauchamp, 2014).

My own sport psychology program development experiences support these conclusions about the link between design success (or failure). In particular, the more attention I have given to organizing the design of the program, the more it has been successfully implemented. Relatedly, more attention has raised the likelihood that relevant stakeholders judge the program to have value and that coaches and administrators show interest in the program's continuation. These experiences underscore, therefore, the importance of the task of organizing a program design before it is implemented.

Organizing a program design means making sure that the methods, procedures, and materials that are going to be used in the program align with the program purpose and goals and that they are configured in a way that allows for successful implementation. More specifically, before you can implement a sport psychology program, the program organization needs to occur in a systematic and thoughtful manner. When the program is organized in a way that pays attention to detail and context, it provides a solid structure that will make the program capable of being implemented, judged as valuable, and continued sustainably.

Toward those ends, here are four steps to take in organizing the design of a sport psychology program:

1. For each goal of the program, identify and then select the methods, materials, and activities that will be used by staff and others who will be implementing the program and that they will use to attain the program goal.
2. Based on the methods, materials, and activities selected for use in the program, decide if it makes sense to configure the program by components or phases.
3. Make certain that those individuals who are going to be implementing the program and who, therefore, will use the above methods, materials, and activities, are qualified and prepared to do so.
4. Plan how the program will be evaluated.

The remainder of the chapter will provide a more detailed description of each of these steps for organizing a program design.

Identifying and Selecting Methods, Materials, and Activities

Essential aspects of any sport psychology program are the methods, materials, and activities that comprise it. Both those implementing the program (its staff) and the participants of the program (athletes, coaches, or another type of program participant) use these methods, materials, and activities.

Methods can be defined as a specific and purposeful way of doing something with those who will be participating in the program. Examples of such methods are goal-setting guidelines, visualization procedures, energy activation steps, relaxation and centering processes, group instruction, and discussion. A method consists of knowledge and technique, and it is applied by staff with program participants.

Materials refers to tangible products and equipment that are also used as part of the program. Examples of program materials are worksheets, computers, books, manuals, and other such products.

Activities pertain to the experiences in which program participants are involved through the use of particular methods and materials.

You can take several approaches to identify and select methods, materials, and activities that will constitute the design of your program, including review of relevant literature, consulting with subject matter experts and colleagues, and the VAK challenge.

Review of Relevant Literature

Relevant sport and performance psychology literature functions as one place to identify methods, materials, and activities for a program. You may find a review of published empirical research and reported program evaluations that discuss programs similar in nature and scope to the purpose and goals of the program you are organizing and designing. In considering this published research, here are some guiding questions:

- Have the methods, materials, and activities you have been studying as you review the research or program evaluations been implemented with groups that are similar to the characteristics and needs of your program's anticipated recipients?

- Are the purpose and goals of the research or program evaluations that you are considering similar in nature and scope to the purpose and goals of the program that you are organizing and designing?
- Do the research or program evaluations describe the methods, materials, and activities in sufficient detail so that you can make an informed choice whether to use all or some of it for your program?
- Why are these methods, materials, and activities applicable to the program that you are designing?

Do not be all that surprised, though, if you are unable to find much precise information about methods, materials, and activities as you review literature. Because the program you are designing is customized to the unique needs and context of a particular group of program participants as well as a specific organization and its related context, the literature may not correspond directly to your work. However, reviews of relevant literature, especially empirical research and published program evaluations, can be effective aides to help you identify and select methods, materials, and activities for your program.

Consulting with Subject Matter Experts and Colleagues

Subject matter experts are sport and performance psychology practitioners and researchers who have particular expertise in the content areas your program will address. Their expertise may apply to the mental and emotional needs of your potential program participants, to the purpose and goals of the proposed program, or to specific methods and materials you may incorporate into the sport psychology program. If you do contact subject matter experts for consultation, I suggest that you make clear with them the following:

- You would like their thoughts and suggestions about methods, materials, and activities for the program you are designing. As such, you are seeking them out as a subject matter expert.
- You would like to know their opinions about specific methods that you are considering for your program, given its nature and scope.
- You want to know if they are aware of programs that are similar in nature and scope to the one that you are in the process of organizing and designing.

Naturally, you also can consult with colleagues who may have designed and implemented similar programs and who want to spend time discussing their suggestions about methods, materials, and activities for your program. In so doing, you can address with them the same three matters that are delineated above in the section on review of relevant literature.

The VAK Challenge

I have found this approach the most helpful for identifying and selecting methods, materials, and activities for programs that I have organized and designed. The approach involves mentally and emotionally "stepping back," then challenging yourself to examine whether you have considered all possible methods, materials, and activities for use as part of the program. In some respects, it is akin to what I call thinking outside the programmatic box.

This approach rests on the VAK framework: Visual, Auditory, and Kinesthetic (see Figure 9.1). The approach involves asking yourself the following questions and then acting on your answers:

- V: *Visual* – What methods, materials, and activities that emphasize the use of the visual modality are available or reasonably can be created? How can you use them in the design of the program?
- A: *Auditory* – How can you leverage the auditory modality (particularly the act of listening by program participants) in the identification, selection, and creation of methods, materials, and activities for the design of the program?
- K: *Kinesthetic* – In what ways can you use the kinesthetic modality— that is, physical action by program participants—as part of the design of the program with regard to identification, selection, and creation of methods, materials, and activities?

V<small>isual</small>    A<small>uditory</small>   K<small>inesthetic</small>

Figure 9.1 VAK framework.

Creating Components and Phases for the Design of the Program

Once you have made decisions about the methods, materials, and activities for the sport psychology program, you can consider whether the program should be further organized by components or by phases.

Program Components

A program component is a part of the program that includes methods, materials, and activities that address one or more of the program goals that are similar in nature and scope. For example, if the program includes goals related to development and increase of knowledge and understanding—that is, educational goals—then a knowledge or educational component of the program may be in order. Alternatively, if the program includes goals that focus on skill acquisition and development, then a skill component may be useful as part of the program design.

The advantage of organizing the design of the program by components is that each component serves to make clear what program goals the program is addressing. In addition, a component serves to indicate the methods, materials, and activities you will use so that program participants can attain those particular goals.

Program Phases

A program phase is used when the methods, materials, and activities of the program occur at different points in time over the course of the program. Thus, a phase of the program aligns with particular goals, methods, and activities that must occur before another phase of the program commences. For instance, an assessment phase of a program may take place before the intervention phase. Similarly, in some programs, an educational phase transpires before a skill development phase.

You should determine whether to organize the design of the program by components or phases, depending on which of the following conditions applies to your program:

- There are distinct sets of goals within the program. For instance, particular goals relate to knowledge, while other goals focus on skills and abilities. The sets of goals are distinct in nature and scope from one another (components).

- There are distinct aspects of the program that occur sequentially, one following another, over the course of time (phases).

Preparing the Implementers of the Program

Another task you must undertake and complete as part of the sport psychology program development process involves preparing those who will be involved in implementing the program. The task begins, of course, with identifying those who will function as program implementers. Depending on the nature and scope of the program, these individuals may be referred to as staff, program consultants, or other titles. I recommend that once you identify these individuals and they agree to be part of the program, they should be involved with you in the following tasks: orientation to the program, clarification of the 3Rs, and training.

Orientation to the Program

This task includes discussing and reviewing the purpose and goals of the program with the program implementers. You should also address the rationale for the program (needs of the program participants) and its methods, materials, and activities, as well as its components or phases. In addition, discuss how you expect the program implementers to fit within and contribute to the program.

Clarification of the 3Rs

Based on the program implementers' orientation to the program, you will accomplish this task by discussing the following with them. First, address their *Roles* in the program, including their future titles. Second, explain their *Responsibilities* in the program, particularly what they are expected to do and accomplish. If the program is complex and large in nature and scope, it is wise to construct a written job or position description for each program implementer. Third, clarify their *Relationships* to others in the program, including to whom they will report (supervisor), and explicate how they will interact with the recipients of the program.

Training

For various sport psychology programs, it will be necessary to provide some form of training for the program implementers. Involving them in training activities is important when these individuals need to learn or refine specific skills they will be using during the program. Likewise, they may need guidance from a trainer to ensure they actually possess the skills needed for them to assist successfully in the implementation of the program.

Formulating a Program Evaluation Plan

When organizing the program's design, people frequently overlook the task of formulating a plan for evaluating the program. Without due attention to this task, program evaluation quickly becomes an afterthought following the program's implementation. At that point, it may be too late to plan and conduct a meaningful program evaluation. When program evaluation ends up on the "back burner" due to a lack of a program evaluation plan, any evaluations that are conducted tend to lack relevance and do not result in information for continued program improvement.

A program evaluation plan serves as the means for obtaining information about the program's implementation and outcomes. A program evaluation will provide useful information for making decisions about the value of the program. It also supplies information that can be used for the continued development and improvement of the program (Maher, 2012).

Although several upcoming chapters will cover the nature and scope of sport psychology program evaluation in detail, I want to emphasize here that you will reap the benefits of program evaluation most by making program evaluation part of the design of the program. For now, suffice it to say that a sport psychology program evaluation plan includes the following elements:

- Description of the program design (e.g., purpose, goals, methods, materials, activities).
- Program evaluation questions (e.g., how was the program implemented? To what degree were goals attained?).
- Methods and procedures for answering the questions (e.g., player reaction survey, goal attainment rating scale).
- Mode for communicating evaluation information and to whom (e.g., written, oral).

Professional Practice Exercises

1. A director of athletics asks you to provide them with information about the sport psychology program that you are going to

implement. How would you proceed with this request, and what information would you provide the athletic director?

2. Recall the sport psychology programs that you have designed or with which you have been involved. What kind of efforts were expended in organizing the design of the program? What went well? What did not go well, and what could have been done better?

10

PUTTING THE PROGRAM DESIGN INTO AN EVALUABLE FORM

The purpose of this chapter is to provide guidelines so that you can design your sport psychology program in such a way that it can be monitored and then evaluated. First, the chapter offers a rationale for placing the program design into an evaluable form and delineates the indicators of "an evaluable program." Second, it discusses the process for conducting an evaluability assessment of the program's design. Third, it supplies guidelines for documenting and communicating an evaluable program design based on evaluability assessment findings.

Rationale for an Evaluable Program Design

The design of a sport psychology program can be compared to a blueprint for building a house (Maher, 2011). Similar to a blueprint, the design of a sport psychology program outlines why the program is necessary (purpose and goals); what is to be implemented (methods, materials, and activities); and how to determine if the implementation of the program is having desired and valuable outcomes for program participants (evaluation plan).

In order to make informed decisions and judgments about why the program has been designed, the program needs to be evaluated in terms of participant reactions and goal attainment, among other matters (Joint Committee on Standards for Educational Evaluation, 1994). For this to happen in a meaningful way, the program design needs to be in an evaluable form.

Given this task, I have relied on the concept of "evaluable program design." An evaluable program design should make explicit the following indicators—in documented form—before the program is implemented:

- *Logic of the Program* – This indicator links the participants' needs with the program's purposes and goals; it also connects the purposes and goals with the program's methods, materials, and activities.
- *Process of the Program* – This indicator addresses the when, where, how, and by whom questions regarding the program's implementation.
- *Content of the Program* – This indicator signifies what the program covers in terms of sport psychology content.
- *Program Evaluation Plan* – This indicator constitutes a plan for how the program will be monitored and evaluated.

An evaluable program design for a sport psychology program provides the following advantages:

- An evaluable program design allows for the documentation of relevant aspects of the program: its logic, process, content, and plan for evaluation.
- It sets the stage for effective communication about the program with program participants, implementers, and others who have a stake in the program's value to participants and to the organization.
- An evaluable program design provides clear and concise information about the nature and scope of the program that will be implemented.
- It also creates a transparency when the program is communicated to others such as those who will receive the program and other stakeholders.

The disadvantages, or drawbacks, of not having a program design that is evaluable include the following:

- The nature and scope of the program—that is, its logic, process, content, and plan for evaluation—will not be clear to those involved in the program or who otherwise have a stake in it.
- Lack of clarity about the design of the program increases the likelihood that the program will not be implemented as planned, nor will

it be able to be sustained over time, even if it is shown to have value for program participants.

- Not having an evaluable program design will deter or otherwise limit monitoring of program implementation and curtail any efforts at program evaluation.
- Without an evaluable program design, communication about the program to program participants, program implementers, and other relevant stakeholders may be compromised.

How do you decide whether the program that you are designing is in an evaluable form in terms of its design? Start with conducting an evaluability assessment of the design of the program.

Conducting an Evaluability Assessment

An evaluability assessment is the process of determining the soundness of the sport psychology program design so that the design can be implemented, monitored, and evaluated successfully. In essence, an evaluability assessment allows you to determine the evaluability of the program you are designing. More specifically, an evaluability assessment should ask whether you have done the following with regard to the program design elements:

1. Identified and described the *program participants* in terms of their important characteristics.
2. Assessed the mental and emotional *needs* of the program participants.
3. Determined the *relevant context* of the program.
4. Established the *purpose* of the program.
5. Created specific, measurable, attainable, relevant, and time-framed *goals* for the program.
6. *Organized* the program in a logical and sequential way with regard to methods, materials, and activities as well as any phases or components.
7. Identified, oriented, and trained the program *staff*.
8. Specified the *location* of the program and the length of time that the program will be in operation.
9. Delineated the *budget* for the program.
10. Formulated a *plan for evaluation* of the program.

Table 10.1 Evaluability assessment form

	Yes	No	Incomplete	Documented
Identified and described participants				
Assessed needs				
Determined relevant context				
Established purpose				
Created goals				
Organized program				
Identified, oriented, and trained staff				
Specified locale and duration				
Delineated the budget				
Formulated an evaluation plan				

To the extent that all of these above ten program design elements are clear, logical, and have been documented (placed in written form), you can consider the design evaluable. If any of the above program design elements are unclear or unknown, then this is the time to obtain the missing information about those elements and to decide how you will procure the necessary information.

Table 10.1 provides a sample of an evaluability assessment form.

Constructing a Program Design Document

Once you have the necessary information (based on the guidelines provided above), then you are ready to construct a program design document. A program design document is a written product that is used to communicate information about the program to those who will be involved with it. This includes the program participants, its implementers, and any program consultants, as well as athletic administrators or executives. A program design document, however, is not a program manual or a curriculum guide. It does not have to be very detailed, just clear enough so that all concerned can understand what the program is and is not.

Using the information that you have generated from an evaluability assessment, a program design document will detail the following about the sport psychology program:

- Title of the program.
- Organization in which the program will be implemented, including any sponsors of the program.

- Oversight for the implementation of the program.
- Location of the program.
- Time frame during which the program will occur.
- Program participants.
- The mental and emotional needs of participants that the program will address.
- Purpose and goals of the program.
- Program organization: the sequencing of program content, including methods, materials, and activities.
- Program personnel (staff, consultants, and others).
- Program budget.
- Program evaluation plan.

Example of a Sport Psychology Program Design that is Evaluable

Appendix A provides an example from my own professional practice of a sport psychology program that is evaluable. Appendix A is a program design from a mental performance rehabilitation program for professional baseball players.

Professional Practice Exercises

1. A director of sports medicine asks you to design a program for student-athletes who have been involved in long-term physical rehabilitation. The student-athletes (i.e., the program participants) are identified, and you or someone else has assessed the needs of these student-athletes to be able to cope in an effective manner with the demands of their rehabilitation. How would you proceed with keeping the director informed about the design of the program?

2. From your experiences in applied sport psychology, what do you consider to be the drawbacks to placing a sport psychology program into an evaluable form, such as this chapter has covered? How would you justify the time and effort you will devote to designing an evaluable program to others who have a stake in the program?

PART IV
IMPLEMENTATION PHASE

Facilitating Program Implementation
Monitoring the Process of Program Implementation

Clarification → Design → Implementation → Evaluation

11

FACILITATING PROGRAM IMPLEMENTATION

The purpose of this chapter is to provide guidelines for ensuring that the sport psychology program you designed starts well and will be implemented as designed. This task is called facilitating program implementation. First, the chapter offers a rationale for the importance of this task. Second, the chapter outlines a framework consisting of seven human factors that can facilitate program implementation of sport psychology programs. Finally, it describes how you can address each of the seven factors to generate an optimal start for your sport psychology program.

Rationale for Facilitating the Implementation of a Sport Psychology Program

Considerable time and effort goes into designing a sport psychology program, including placing the program into an evaluable form that can be implemented and evaluated (see Chapter 10 for an evaluable program design). In light of the amount of time and effort that goes into program design, it would be disappointing, to say the least, if the sport psychology program you have designed could not start when it was supposed to begin and could not sustain itself over the course of time. Accordingly, you should give attention to ensuring that the program commences and that it happens in accord with your program design.

The advantage of the successful completion of the task of facilitating program implementation is that it places you in a better position to ensure that the program you designed will become operational in the way that you intended. Without purposeful attention to facilitating program implementation, the program realistically may not begin, may not occur according to the program design, or may fizzle out (Damschroeder et al., 2009).

Over the years, I have been involved with the task of facilitating program implementation, and I have learned much about how to engage practically and successfully as I undertake and complete this task. No matter how large or small the particular program, I have found the best way to help facilitate the implementation of sport psychology programs: the DURABLE factors. Using this acronym, I have organized the facilitating program implementation task based on seven human factors. The rest of this chapter is dedicated to explaining these DURABLE factors for facilitating program implementation.

The DURABLE Factors

Over the years, I have researched and conducted the task of program implementation not only with my own programs in sport and performance psychology, but also with other programs in education, human services, and business settings. Based on my investigations and professional experiences with program implementation, I have identified seven factors under your control as the sport psychology program consultant. You can use them to help your program launch smoothly.

I have labeled these factors with an acronym as the DURABLE factors (visually portrayed in Figure 11.1). I first will introduce the seven factors briefly before turning to a more detailed description of each factor. The DURABLE factors for facilitating sport psychology program implementation are the following:

1. D – *Discuss* the sport psychology program you designed with those who will be involved in the program or who otherwise have a stake in it.
2. U – *Understand* the concerns of those who will be affected by the program's implementation.
3. R – *Reinforce* the behaviors of program participants and program implementers.

```
Discuss
Understand
Reinforce
Acquire
Build
Learn
Execute
```

Figure 11.1 The DURABLE factors.

4. A – *Acquire* the approvals and resources necessary for the program to be implemented according to the program design.
5. B – *Build* positive expectations about the program's implementation and its value for program participants.
6. L – *Learn* about the people who are part of the program.
7. E – *Execute* the design of the program.

If you choose to engage in and address these factors, all of them will be under your cognitive and behavioral control as a practitioner.

Discuss *the Sport Psychology Program*

If you have given time and effort to designing a sport psychology program, it would be a mistake not to discuss the program with its participants and those otherwise affected by it. Depending on the nature and scope of the program, these individuals and groups may include: (a) the athletes who will be the focus of the program; (b) the individuals who will be implementing the program, including program staff and consultants; (c) coaches and support staff members in the athletic department; (d) athletic administrators; and (e) other relevant stakeholders, such as parents.

It is best to discuss the program with these individuals and groups in real time and in person rather than via email or text. Real-time discussion through face-to-face meetings or (at least) conference calls allows you to be frank about the program, to clarify concerns, and to respond to questions.

Such discussion also indicates that you consider the individuals and groups—and their input—important to the program even before it begins.

A program discussion meeting does not have to be long in terms of minutes: a well-planned half-hour meeting may very well suffice. If at all possible, you should plan this kind of meeting in advance and not allow it to occur at the last minute. Here is a general approach and format for a productive program discussion meeting:

- Schedule a date, time, and location of the meeting that works for all parties.
- Provide attendees with a brief description of the program that includes information about the athletes or others who will be participating in the program, the purpose and goals of the program, and the organization of the program in terms of its design. In this regard, the program design document is an invaluable resource to share with the attendees to foster fruitful discussion.
- Request that recipients of the material review it prior to the meeting.
- At the discussion meeting itself, you can use or otherwise adapt the following agenda:
  - Discuss the rationale for the program, including the needs it addresses.
  - Present the purpose and goals of the program and explain why these outcomes are important for program participants. Ask for questions and clarification of the purpose and goals.
  - Review the program's organization in detail in order to demonstrate how the program will actualize its purpose and goals. This includes elucidating methods, materials, activities, times, dates, and locations of the program. Ask for questions and clarification.
  - Consider matters of confidentiality for those who will participate in the program.
  - Introduce or otherwise comment on the individuals implementing the program (staff, consultants, and others), and clarify your own role.

Understand *the Concerns about the Program*

I have found that whenever a sport psychology program is about to be implemented, apparent and latent questions and concerns arise from various people, such as program participants, implementers, and administrators.

Whatever the circumstance may be, such concerns should not go unaddressed. Rather, you should seek to discover and comprehend the concerns individuals and groups hold regarding the program. Giving attention to their concerns and questions should help you avert problems and provide answers to the questions participants and others may raise.

By seeking to understand people's concerns about the program, you also will convey the message that even before the program is implemented, you want the program to work for them. It demonstrates that you want to know them and that you care about their concerns. One approach to grasping people's concerns involves asking for questions during a discussion about the program. Be sincere in your interest in their questions, and provide the best responses you can at the time. Similarly, you may find that pursuing further contact with individuals or small groups may allow you to understand more clearly the questions that athletes, coaches, and others pose to you.

There are any number of concerns that those involved in a sport psychology program may raise. Thus, I share here some particular concerns that people who have participated or otherwise have a stake in sport psychology programs have shared with me. They are concerned that:

- If they do not participate in the program, their position on a team or in the organization may be jeopardized.
- What they say or do in the program will be reported back to a coach or to an athletic administrator.
- The program will take too much time.
- Their performance will be evaluated based on how they participated in the program.
- The staff conducting the program have not played their sport and do not understand the context of the sport.

Anticipating and understanding concerns like these in advance of the program's implementation allows you to take action. For instance, if the concerns are about the program design, you can use those particular concerns to improve the design.

Reinforce *Behaviors Associated with Successful Program Implementation*

Successful program implementation (that is, a program that has been implemented according to its program design) requires that those involved in implementing the program engage in specific actions and behavior related to their roles and responsibilities. These actions and behaviors include: (a) attending meetings to discuss the program; (b) completing forms and checklists that are used to establish baseline information about program participants; (c) being involved in program training sessions; (d) following through on commitments related to the program; (e) informing those conducting the program about their opinions and concerns; and (f) other necessary actions and behaviors.

In order to reinforce such actions and behaviors, you should provide positive response and feedback to program participants and program staff. In my experience, I have found that people have responded well—that is, received the actions positively and maintained their good behavior—to particular actions. Thus, I recommend that you try the following reinforcements:

- Thank them both verbally and in written form for engaging in desired behaviors.
- Let them know that you appreciate their completion of forms and checklists.
- Give feedback on their attendance at meetings as indicative of their professionalism and of their commitment to being a good teammate.
- Tell them you have appreciated their feedback about the program.
- Periodically provide them with some tangible reinforcements for program involvement (such as having food available at or after a program session).
- Offer other relevant positive reinforcements, depending on the program and context.

Acquire *Approvals and Resources*

Most sport psychology programs that I helped to design and implement—and that were successful at sustaining themselves—have had explicit authorization as well as resources devoted to them. These resources typically have come from individuals in some position of authority (such as general managers, athletic directors, and coaches). However, without the approval and resources from those in power, the program's implementation may be undermined or otherwise curtailed. Thus, I suggest you actively seek explicit endorsement from those in authority or those overseeing the program, even if you believe they implicitly support the program.

For instance, you may ask the appropriate individual to send an email or letter to participants, implementers, and other relevant stakeholders. You can encourage the ones in authority to meet with the individuals or groups to underscore their approval and support for the program. They also can be encouraged to meet with these individuals as a sign of sanction and support for the program.

In addition, I recommend that you do everything possible to certify that the resources needed for the program to be implemented according to program design have been acquired or otherwise enacted. Nothing can be more exasperating and frustrating than not having the resources in place to implement the program that you have designed and are ready to launch according to schedule. The resources you will need include, but are not limited to, the following:

- *Human Resources* – Staff have been selected, oriented, and trained.
- *Informational Resources* – An evaluable program design has been formulated and documented.
- *Technological Resources* – Materials, computers, and other things are in place.
- *Physical Resources* – Necessary meeting rooms and offices are available.
- *Financial Resources* – Funds to support program implementation have been procured.

Assuring the availability of these resources is essential because nothing can undermine a program or delay its start more than if the resources to operate the program are missing or inaccessible.

Build *Positive Expectations about the Program*

In order for any sport psychology program to start successfully and sustain itself, the people who are involved in it (particularly program implementers and consultants) need to be positive about the program. After all, without the various stakeholders' positive and enthusiastic attitude toward the program, the program may fail to be implemented as designed or may not be able to sustain its operations once implemented. In contrast, when people manifest positive expectations and enthusiasm about the program, the likelihood increases that the program will be implemented as intended.

Here are some approaches for building positive expectations about a sport psychology program:

- Pay attention to the staff of the program, not just as program implementers but also as people. Make them feel appreciated.
- When speaking with athletes about the program, mention that other athletes who have participated in the program deemed it valuable. Assure them that you expect the program to be valuable to them, too.
- Whenever interacting with individuals or groups who will be involved or otherwise affected by the program, let them know why you personally are excited about the program.
- Be ready to speak about the program when you are asked to do so. Do not suppress your enthusiasm: make yourself available to anyone interested in the program, such as athletic department officials and (when appropriate) the media.

Learn *about the People Who Will Be Part of the Program*

Whenever I have taken the time to get to know the individuals who are going to be involved in the program and its implementation—to know them as people, over and above their program roles—the more we all have benefitted. What I have learned about and from them has helped us to get their program started and to sustain it successfully.

Learning about the people who will be part of the program includes getting to know them on a personal level, rather than just as someone who is involved in the program. This requires getting to know their names and the roles and responsibilities they hold; it involves finding out how they would like to be addressed and what they think about sports and other things important to them. You should seek to learn not only about the athletes who will be the program's target population, but also their coaches, program staff, and other relevant stakeholders.

However, deepening the interpersonal relationships that occur in your program context, as I have described above, does not mean that you pry and seek personal information. For instance, you should not give them a form to complete or conduct a formal one-on-one interview to learn about their lives. Rather, what I am encouraging is your best attempt to develop a rapport and trust with them, preferably in an informal manner. In a sincere way, your task is to allow them to perceive you as someone interested in them as you manifest a professional care for them in light of your role, theirs, and the relevant context. After all, unless the athletes and others who are going to be involved in the program believe that you care for them, they may very well not care what you or the program has to offer.

Execute *the Design of the Program*

This factor has to do with being ready, willing, and able to execute the design of the program—and to do so in a manner that exudes confidence and enthusiasm. More specifically, a successful execution involves paying attention to detail as described in the program design.

Here are some actions and behaviors that allow for successful execution and, thus, implementation of the program:

- Making sure that roles and responsibilities are clear to all concerned.
- Confirming that schedules, rooms, and other matters are in place for the start of the program.
- Informing those who are going to be involved in the program about their expected responsibilities (e.g., punctuality for program sessions and meetings, timely submission of reports or other requests for information, and articulating any questions they may have).
- Committing to the task of program implementation without self-judgment and with confidence.

Professional Practice Exercises

1. Based on your experiences to date with preparing a sport psychology program for implementation, what have you done well that contributed to the program being implemented as expected? How does what you did in those cases compare to other times that you may not have put in enough time to prepare the program for implementation?
2. You have developed a sport psychology program that you believe is capable of being implemented successfully. However, you are not quite sure that the program will get off the ground and feel that something is missing. How would you proceed?

12

MONITORING THE PROCESS OF PROGRAM IMPLEMENTATION

The purpose of this chapter is to provide guidelines to help you monitor the implementation process of the sport psychology program you designed, particularly in relation to its program design. First, the chapter presents a rationale for monitoring the process of sport psychology program implementation. Second, it addresses how to monitor the process of program implementation using a process control approach. Third, it describes methods for monitoring the process of sport psychology program implementation.

Rationale for Monitoring the Process of Program Implementation

Monitoring program implementation is part of the Implementation Phase of the sport psychology program development process. This monitoring task focuses on what happens to the program once it is in operation, that is, during the process of its implementation. More specifically, such program implementation process monitoring seeks to determine whether things are occurring according to expectations following implementation.

As any program is implemented—including sport psychology programs—many unexpected matters can arise and affect its process. The unanticipated happenings may include issues such as failure to use methods and activities or to address particular program goals. You may also have problems with program participants not attending the planned sessions (Durlak & DuPre,

2008). When the process of program implementation varies from what was expected (especially in relation to the program design), those variations may require making adjustments in the program as it is being implemented.

The monitoring of the process of the implementation of a sport psychology program is important for several reasons, particularly the following:

- A sport psychology program is expected to proceed according to its design. This is important because considerable thought, time, and effort have been given to formulating a program design and getting it ready for implementation. In order to determine whether the program is proceeding according to program design, the process of program implementation merits monitoring.
- In order to decide whether a sport psychology program is being implemented as designed, you can establish process control limits. Process control limits offer a way for you to increase your accuracy as you judge whether the program is aligned or misaligned with the expected process. (Process control and process control limits will be discussed in a later section of this chapter.)
- While a sport psychology program is being implemented, it is likely you will need to make adjustments in one or more program design elements. An important point of reference for making these adjustments is the process that the program was intended to take. Once you compare the intended process to the actual process occurring, you can determine the kinds of adjustments and revisions you need to make to the program.
- You can use the information generated from program implementation process monitoring for program evaluation purposes when that time arrives.

How to Monitor the Process of Program Implementation

In order to monitor the process of the implementation of a sport psychology program effectively, it is necessary to understand the design of the program. If you have followed the guidelines in the chapters on program design, you will have a program design that is capable of being evaluated and monitored. (Remember, this is termed an *evaluable program design*.)

When you understand the design of the program (and it is evaluable), you are in a position to recognize how each program design element should be implemented. You particularly will know how to consider such implementation from a process perspective. However, if you do not know the design of the program, or it is not in an evaluable form, then your monitoring of the program implementation process is likely to be fruitless.

In contrast, once you know the design of the program and it has been documented as an evaluable program design, you can undertake eight program implementation process monitoring tasks. These tasks involve monitoring the following:

1. Whether the appropriate athletes or other program participants are attending the program.
2. If the program's purpose and goals are being addressed by means of methods and activities.
3. The extent to which those involved in the program are adhering to the program's policies and procedures.
4. If methods, materials, equipment, and facilities are being utilized as anticipated.
5. The degree to which the components and phases of the program align with program design.
6. If the budget for the program is being expended in an appropriate manner.
7. The extent to which program personnel are performing their roles and responsibilities.
8. Whether program evaluation activities are occurring as planned.

Key Notions and Terms

The rest of the chapter will focus on these tasks with regard to the task of program process monitoring, program process control, and process control limits. Before proceeding, I need to clarify my terms:

- *Program Process Monitoring* – Determining whether the process of the program occurs according to program design as the program is being implemented.
- *Process Control* – Ensuring that the program process stays within the limits of what it was intended to do (with due recognition that there always will be some variation in the program).
- *Process Control Limits* – Involving the extent to which the program does not follow its intended course.

- *Process Control Limit Indicators* – Benchmarks that allow you to make judgments about whether and to what extent the process exceeds its intended limits.
- *Process Control Monitoring Methods* – The means for gathering data and making judgments about the implementation of the program.

Implementation Monitoring Tasks

The remainder of this chapter provides a process control framework for each of the eight monitoring tasks mentioned above. As you consider this framework, note that the examples I use are generic and, as such, do not refer to any particular program. Rather, these generic examples are based on my professional practice in developing sport psychology programs at professional and collegiate levels. Furthermore, the nature, scope, and size of your program, as described in its particular program design, will determine what aspects of this process control framework you will use for your program.

Table 12.1 is a chart of the implementation process monitoring tasks; the remaining sections of the chapter will focus on them.

Table 12.1 Monitoring process of program implementation

	According to program design	Not according to program design	Both according to and not according to design	Comments
Participant attendance				
Purposes and goal addressed by methods and activities				
Policies and procedures being followed				
Methods, materials, equipment, and facilities being utilized				
Components and phases occurring as planned				
Budget expended appropriately				
Program personnel performing roles and responsibilities				
Program evaluation activities occurring as planned				

Monitor Whether the Appropriate Athletes are Participating in the Program

Process Control Limit Indicators

- *Upper Control Limit* – There are athletes participating in the program who are not supposed to be in it.
- *Lower Control Limit* – There are athletes who should be in the program but who are not participating in it.

Process Control Monitoring Methods

- Review of program registration and attendance records.
- Reports or comments provided by the coordinator of the program or made by staff implementing the program regarding the actual attendees.

Monitor Whether the Methods and Activities are Addressing the Program's Purpose and Goals

Process Control Limit Indicators

- *Upper Control Limit* – Other goals that were not stated in the program design are being addressed.
- *Lower Control Limit* – All or some of the goals of the program are not being addressed.

Process Control Monitoring Methods

- Review of program reports and materials that are being used in the program.
- Interviews and discussions with those who are implementing the program.

Monitor Whether the Policies and Procedures of the Program are Being Followed

Process Control Limit Indicators

- *Upper Control Limit* – The program's policies and procedures are not being applied, thereby allowing ineligible athletes to take part in the program or precluding those who are supposed to be in the program from attending.

- *Lower Control Limit* – Policies and procedures are being applied in a restricted manner and not in a way that was intended. This rigidity creates challenges for consistently applying the policies and procedures.

Process Control Monitoring Methods

- Review of the application of policies and procedures as part of supervision sessions or discussions with program implementers.
- Review of program reports.

Monitor Whether Methods, Materials, Equipment, and Facilities are Being Utilized

Process Control Limit Indicators

- *Upper Control Limit* – The program's methods, materials, equipment, and/or facilities are being overly used, more so than appropriate.
- *Lower Control Limit* – The program's methods, materials, equipment, and/or facilities are being used less than expected.

Process Control Monitoring Methods

- Review of program records and reports.
- Comments from program implementers.
- Direct observation of the implementation of the program.

Monitor the Extent to Which the Components and Phases of the Program are Occurring

Process Control Limit Indicators

- *Upper Control Limit* – The program's components or phases are occurring too loosely and not according to the program design plan.
- *Lower Control Limit* – The program's components or phases are occurring in too restrictive a manner, thereby failing to address specific aspects of the program.

Process Control Monitoring Methods

- Review of the records and sessions of the program.
- Comments from the implementers of the program.
- Direct observation of the implementation of the program.

Monitor Whether the Budget for the Program is Being Utilized as Appropriate
Process Control Limit Indicators

- *Upper Control Limit* – The budget is being used for the purchase of items that are not used or included in the program.
- *Lower Control Limit* – The budget is being used too restrictively, resulting in approved and necessary items not being purchased.

Process Control Monitoring Methods

- Review of budgetary expenditures.
- Discussions with program implementers and those who are accountable for the budget of the program.

Monitor Whether the Program Personnel are Performing Their Roles and Responsibilities
Process Control Limit Indicators

- *Upper Control Limit* – Program personnel are engaged in their roles as expected.
- *Lower Control Limit* – Program personnel are engaged in roles that are not ones included as part of the program design.

Process Control Monitoring Methods

- Observation of the performance of program personnel.
- Discussions with program personnel.

Monitor Whether Program Evaluation Activities are Occurring as Planned

Process Control Limit Indicators

- *Upper Control Limit* – Program evaluation activities are occurring in ways that go above and beyond what is part of the program evaluation plan.
- *Lower Control Limit* – Program evaluation activities are not occurring at all.

Process Control Monitoring Methods

- Review of the program evaluation plan.
- Discussions with program implementers and those responsible for program evaluation activities.

Professional Practice Exercises

1. What are the most challenging experiences you have encountered when trying to monitor the process of a sport psychology program? Looking back on these challenges, what might you have done differently in dealing with them?

2. An athletic director asks you to provide a report to them and the executive committee about "how the program is going" and "how it should continue." What would be your response to the athletic director, and how would you provide them with the requested program implementation information?

PART V
EVALUATION PHASE

Formulating a Program Evaluation Plan
Evaluating Program Implementation
Evaluating Goal Attainment
Evaluating Reactions to the Program
Evaluating the Program's Strong Points and Limitations
Communicating and Using Program Evaluation Information
Closing Comments and Program Development Practice Standards

Clarification ➤ Design ➤ Implementation ➤ **Evaluation**

13
FORMULATING A PROGRAM EVALUATION PLAN

This chapter delineates guidelines for formulating a program evaluation plan for a sport psychology program. Using a formulated plan for evaluating a sport psychology program allows you to obtain evaluative information about various aspects of your program, including the attainment of program goals, reactions to the program, and program strong points and limitations. In turn, this evaluative information will enable you to make decisions regarding the continued development, improvement, and sustainability of the program. Accordingly, this chapter provides a rationale for having a sport psychology program evaluation plan. The chapter next sets forth the criteria for a sport psychology program evaluation plan. Finally, it describes the elements of a program evaluation plan and supplies a program evaluation planning worksheet and an example of a program evaluation plan.

Rationale for a Program Evaluation Plan

A program evaluation plan is an important part of the process of developing a sport psychology program. The evaluative information that is derived from the use of the plan will allow you to make informed judgments and decisions about the continued development, improvement, and sustainability of a sport psychology program (Maher, 2012).

There are several reasons a program evaluation plan—and its experience-informed viewpoint on the program—is vital to your program. First, whatever its nature and scope, a sport psychology program is an investment of resources. These resources include staff, methods, procedures, materials, information, monetary funds, time, physical setting, and location. These and other resources are allocated and then expended so that the program can have value for both its participants and the organization in which it is embedded. Thus, it is necessary to ascertain the extent to which the resources of the program have been utilized and deemed worthwhile (in terms of adding value to the athletes or other program participants). A program evaluation plan serves as the means to make judgments and decisions systematically and objectively about the resources that have been invested in the design and implementation of the program.

Second, a sport psychology program is implemented in time, space, and locale; more often than not, the program occurs over days and weeks. People expect that during this time, the program is being implemented according to its program design. Furthermore, they assume that the program will be developed continuously and improved with regard to its value to program participants. Accordingly, a program evaluation plan functions as a means for successfully undertaking and completing the valuing task and for using the resultant evaluative information for decision-making about the program (Kane, 2013).

Third and relatedly, the formulation and use of a program evaluation plan can address concerns regarding the future. For instance, if a sport psychology program is judged as adding value to program participants in terms of goal attainment, and there are positive reactions about participants' experiences, then the question becomes whether the program should be continued or even expanded to other athletes, teams, or locations. If, however, the sport psychology program is judged as not being of value to program participants, then a decision can be made as to whether the program should be ended or otherwise adjusted.

Fourth, those who are responsible for funding the program should understand the sport psychology program that has been designed and implemented. Therefore, it is important to provide program funders and related stakeholders (such as sports administrators) with useful information about the current status of the program, particularly regarding the program's judged value for its participants. A program evaluation plan can provide this evaluative information in a way that has meaning for key program stakeholders.

Criteria for a Sport Psychology Program Evaluation Plan

A program evaluation plan serves as the foundation for program evaluation activities. I recommend that this plan should be well thought-out. You should also give it concerted professional attention, because formulating a program evaluation plan is professional time very well spent.

A sport psychology program evaluation plan should meet four criteria. These criteria are:

1. Practicality
2. Utility
3. Propriety
4. Technical Defensibility.

Here are descriptions for each of these criteria:

- *Practicality* – A program evaluation plan is *practical* if it can be implemented in the organization in a way that does not disrupt the routines of that organization. This includes not interfering in athletes' preparation for competition, in ongoing team practices, and in the daily schedules and logistics of the organization.
- *Utility* – A program evaluation plan is *useful* if the plan generates evaluative information that allows the client, you, and other stakeholders to become informed specifically about a range of programmatic matters related to the development, improvement, and sustainability of the program. These matters include issues such as who actually participated in the program and to what extent; how the program was implemented in relation to the program design; how the program seems to have added value to program participants in terms of goal attainment; and the program's current strong points and limitations.
- *Propriety* – A program evaluation plan is *proper* if it enables evaluation activities to occur in a way that adheres to all relevant legal strictures (such as those of HIPPA), follows standards relating to tests and measurements, and demonstrates compliance with any other relevant rules and regulations.

- *Technical Defensibility* – A program evaluation plan can be considered *technically defensible* if it employs valid evaluation methods, procedures, and instruments, particularly as a means to answer carefully selected program evaluation questions.

Essential Elements of a Sport Psychology Program Evaluation Plan

An evaluation plan for a sport psychology program should be explicit in nature and scope. In that regard, I have found that if you clearly include the following six elements as part of the plan, the plan likely will meet the four criteria described above. Even more, the program evaluation actually may occur.

The six essential elements of a sport psychology program evaluation plan are:

1. Purpose of the program evaluation.
2. Description of the program design.
3. Program evaluation questions.
4. Program evaluation protocol.
5. Confidentiality and related ethical matters.
6. Program evaluation budget.

In the remaining sections of this chapter, I will discuss how you can address each of these essential elements when formulating a sport psychology program evaluation plan which are illustrated visually in Figure 13.1.

Purpose of the Program Evaluation

Program evaluation means different things to different people, including researchers and sport psychology practitioners. For instance, researchers typically are interested in generalizability of results and theory development with regard to a particular domain of inquiry. Thus, program evaluation may be a component of a larger research design or project on which they are working, which is likely to be driven by concerns relating to experimental control and internal and external validity (Patton, 2002).

Practitioners, though, are dealing with real-time clients. Thus, we are driven by the needs of program participants within a particular context, such a specific team in a particular sport and athletic league or conference.

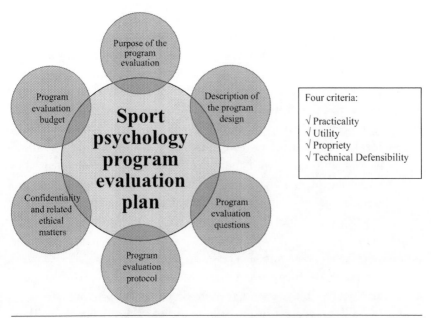

Figure 13.1 Six essential elements of a sport psychology program evaluation plan.

Therefore, program evaluation with regard to professional practice focuses on assessing and making judgments about a particular program so that the program can be developed, improved, and sustained if it is determined to have value. Based on my professional practice in sport and performance psychology—and with specific reference to this book's concentration on the task of developing, improving, and sustaining sport psychology programs— I offer three viewpoints on the purpose of a sport psychology program evaluation.

First, sport psychology program evaluation can be defined as the process of obtaining evaluative information about a clearly described sport psychology program; this evaluation is part of an evaluable program design. This process is enacted so that the resulting evaluative information can be used to assist your client, you, and other relevant stakeholders in making the following kinds of judgments and decisions:

• Understand who participated in the program, how the program was implemented, and the extent to which program goals were attained.

- Learn how those who have participated in the program (e.g., athletes) or those who have otherwise been involved in it (e.g., program staff) have reacted to the program and perceived their experiences with the program.
- Determine the current strong points of the program, such as its ability to be implemented, participants' degree of goal attainment, and program participant reactions.
- Identify areas of the program that currently are limiting its effectiveness and that can benefit from continued development and improvement.
- Decide the next appropriate steps with the program, including whether to continue, expand, or end it.

Second, a program evaluation plan is a necessity in order to obtain evaluative information to render judgments and to foster making appropriate decisions about the program. In this regard, the best time to develop a program evaluation plan is when you are in the process of designing the program. Thus, you should include a program evaluation plan as part of the initial program design.

Third, those responsible for the program's continued development should communicate and use—in a practical, timely, and understandable manner—the evaluative information that is obtained from the activities that are part of the program evaluation plan. For sport psychology practitioners, therefore, the results of the program evaluation have immediate effects on the program itself and thus play an integral role in developing, improving, and sustaining a sport psychology program.

Description of the Program Design

In order to evaluate a sport psychology program in a reasonable and defensible way, a program design is necessary; more simply, an evaluable description of the program is essential. (In Chapter 10, we covered how to organize a sport psychology program, while Chapter 11 discussed how to put the program into an evaluable form.) Proceeding with a vague written or verbal description and without an evaluable program design would be treating the sport psychology program as a "black box," so to speak, in which you don't really know what is inside the program or what it comprises. In other words, without an evaluable description of the program design, it is impossible to make judgments about the program, since it will be unclear what the program is and is not. Therefore, an evaluable program design is the preferred way to describe the program so that it can be evaluated.

In this regard, below are the elements of the design of an evaluable program, which you may recall from Chapter 10. More specifically, a sport psychology program evaluation plan describes the program so that there is no uncertainty about what the program that is going to be evaluated consists of and, alternatively, what is not included as part of the program.

A clear description of a sport psychology program for program evaluation purposes will include the following information about the program:

- Program participants who will be provided the program and who are expected to participate in it.
- Purpose and goals of the program, which are based on the mental and emotional needs of the program participants.
- Organization of the program in terms of components and/or phases.
- Sequence, timing, and use of methods, materials, and activities.
- Staff and consultants who will be involved with the implementation of the program.
- Facilities and location of the program.
- Budget that is necessary to support the implementation of the program.

Program Evaluation Questions

Over the years of my professional practice, I have found the use of program evaluation questions a very useful approach for assisting clients, practitioners, and other relevant stakeholders in understanding the program and in making judgments and decisions about it. I believe the questions are an effective evaluation strategy since posing a question about the program provides an opportunity to answer the question.

A program evaluation question is one that will allow information to be gathered in a practical and technically defensible manner, given the nature and scope of the program. In addition, and most important, your client agrees that the question is one they would like to have answered and that is possible to answer.

In most of the sport and performance psychology programs that I have evaluated, a set of common program evaluation questions have recurred. I have found that answers to these questions have informed me and clients well and have helped us to make wise program planning decisions. These recurring program evaluation questions are:

- To whom was the program provided, and to what extent did they participate in it?
- How was the program implemented in relation to its design?
- What adjustments were made in the program once it was implemented?
- To what extent were the goals of the program attained?
- What were the reactions of participants and others to the program?
- What have been the strong points and limitations of the program?
- What are next steps and actions to take with regard to the program?

All of these program evaluation questions likely cannot be answered as part of any one program evaluation plan. After all, time, data, sanctions, and resources may curtail being able to answer some of them. However, no matter the case, a protocol is necessary in order to answer each and every program evaluation question for any particular sport psychology program. The nature and scope of a program evaluation protocol is discussed next.

Program Evaluation Protocol

A program evaluation protocol is a written document and an important part of the program evaluation plan. In essence, a protocol identifies the program evaluation questions and explicates how these questions will be answered.

A protocol for the evaluation of a sport psychology program details the following:

- The program evaluation questions to be answered.
- The methods, procedures, and instruments that will be used to gather information to answer the questions.
- Methods and procedures for any data analysis.
- Roles and responsibilities for gathering the data to answer the questions.
- Guidelines for the use of the resultant evaluation information.

Confidentiality and Related Ethical Matters

During most program evaluations, including sport psychology program evaluations, individuals are asked to complete questionnaires or rating scales and/or engage in interviews in relation to a program in which they have participated or have otherwise been involved. These individuals may include the athletes who have participated in the program, coaches of the athletes, program evaluation consultants, funders of the program, and others.

As part of the program evaluation plan, you need to make explicit the issue of confidentiality with those who are being requested to provide responses. In this respect, sport psychology practitioners are expected to adhere to a code of professional ethics, particularly the ethics codes of the Association of Applied Sport Psychology and the American Psychological Association. These codes emphasize the confidentiality of the responses of those who provide information about their perceptions and involvement in a program.

As part of a protocol for program evaluation, therefore, athletes and other respondents need to be informed about and assured of the following matters, typically through an informed consent form:

- The reason they are being asked to complete a questionnaire or rating scale or to participate in an interview.
- The individuals who will have access to their responses and in what form they will view the responses (such as aggregate data only).
- Further assurance that their responses to these instruments will be maintained in confidence.
- Their right not to participate in the data collection activities.
- Other relevant matters.

Program Evaluation Budget

A program evaluation involves thought, energy, effort, materials, and time. This underscores the need for a budget for the evaluation. Although people typically may not consider the need for a program evaluation budget, it is important and cannot be dismissed. Without a budget allotment, people may question the need for a program evaluation. However, a defensible program evaluation cannot be conducted without resources and on one's lunch hour, so to speak: you need to include program evaluation in the budget as you plan your program.

You can develop a budget for sport psychology program evaluation by considering the costs associated with the following budget line items:

- Materials for the evaluation, such as assessment instruments and laptops.
- Facilities such as rentals for office and meetings rooms.
- Compensation for program staff and consultants.
- Other relevant items.

Program Evaluation Planning Worksheet

I have found the worksheet shown in Figure 13.2 to be useful in the formulation of a sport psychology program evaluation plan.

See Appendix B for an example of a program evaluation plan; it includes a program evaluation protocol.

Professional Practice Exercises

1. You are asked by an athletic director to evaluate their school's sport psychology programs. How would you discuss this task with the athletic director?

2. What challenges have you discovered in conducting a sport psychology program in your organization? If you have never conducted a sport psychology program evaluation, how would you need to proceed in your setting in order to formulate and carry out a program evaluation plan?

Sport Psychology Program Evaluation Worksheet

[Name of Program] _____   [Client] _____ .

[Description of the Program] (*attached: an evaluable program design*)

_____

_____

1. Purpose and Goals: _____

_____

2. Components/Phases: _____

_____

3. Methods, Materials, and Activities: _____

_____

4. Program Staff: _____

_____

5. Other: _____

_____

Figure 13.2 Program evaluation planning worksheet.

14
EVALUATING PROGRAM IMPLEMENTATION

The purpose of this chapter is to provide guidelines for conducting an evaluation of the implementation of a sport psychology program, following the completion of the program. First, the chapter presents a rationale for why evaluating program implementation is an important part of developing, improving, and sustaining a sport psychology program. Second, it delineates implementation evaluation questions that help focus this form of program evaluation. Third, it covers methods and procedures for obtaining implementation evaluation information. Fourth, the chapter considers how to communicate and use implementation evaluation information.

Rationale for Evaluation of the Implementation of a Sport Psychology Program

The evaluation of the implementation of a sport psychology program is important for several reasons. First, the evaluative information that is obtained regarding how the program was implemented—how it actually occurred—will allow you to judge the extent to which the program conformed to the design of the program. In turn, you can ascertain whether the design of the program was a reasonable one. The evaluative information also will indicate whether the program design will require modification if the program is going to continue to operate in the future (Forman, 2015).

Second, evaluative information concerning the implementation of the program emphatically highlights what the program was and what it was not, following its completion. In this sense, the program itself becomes an important context that needs to be understood, particularly if the organization is going to continue to implement it with the same or other program participants.

Third, when you conduct an evaluation of the implementation of the program, you will have information to share with those in the athletic department and other areas of a sports organization about what the program "looks like" and what was delivered to the athletes who took part in it. I have found, not infrequently, that many of those who work in sport areas at professional and collegiate levels are interested in the context, content, and operation of the program more so than the results.

Implementation Evaluation Questions

There are a number of implementation evaluation questions that you can include as part of a sport psychology program evaluation plan. Answers to implementation evaluation questions will provide you with useful information about the nature and scope of a sport psychology program's implementation. In addition, I have found answers to implementation evaluation questions particularly helpful in deciding what to do next with the program once it has been completed.

Naturally, it may not be possible to answer all of the questions delineated below as part of a sport psychology program evaluation plan. The size and scope of any particular program and the resources available to collect the information may very well limit how many questions your evaluation can address. However, you at least should consider all of the questions below as part of an overall program evaluation plan.

I have included commentary about the following important implementation evaluation questions, which I recommend you consider for your program evaluation plan:

- *To what extent was the sport psychology program implemented according to its design?* Of course, this question can only be answered if there is an evaluable program design, such as the kind covered in Chapter 10 (placing the program into an evaluable form). An answer to this question, though, will allow you not only to document what has occurred but also to increase your understanding about why the program was or was not implemented according to design.

- *Have the components or phases of the program occurred as anticipated?* This question is important for those sport psychology programs organized by phases or components, where activities are expected to occur in a prescribed sequence and when the timing of those activities is important in terms of goal attainment. It is not unusual, however, for multi-component and multi-phase programs to have the tendency to go off-track (Forman, 2015). In these circumstances, some program activities that are supposed to happen at a particular time do not come to fruition. Your evaluative information thus will allow you to trouble-shoot what did not occur in sequence and to determine reasons why.

- *Did the intended participants for the program receive the program and participate in it?* You should never assume that the athletes or others who were supposed to receive and participate in a sport psychology program actually were involved in it. There can be many reasons why participants do not attend a program or drop out of it. Therefore, the answer to this implementation evaluation question will provide leads as to what happened to attendance and participation; it may also indicate why some or all of the athletes or others did not receive or participate in the program.

- *Has the content of the program been covered in an appropriate manner?* The content of the program, as reflected in the goals of the program, was developed to meet particular program goals. The implementation evaluation information therefore can help you determine the extent to which program goals have been attained and whether the program includes appropriate content to achieve the goals.

- *Have methods and materials been used in an appropriate way?* This implementation evaluation question is similar to but slightly different from the question about program content. If specific methods and materials were supposed to be used in the program, then this answer will reveal if those methods and materials actually were used. This especially will be helpful for future decision-making if the program is going to be implemented again.

- *Have program personnel followed through with their roles and respon- sibilities with regard to the design of the program?* This implementa- tion evaluation question should not be equated to a performance evaluation question, which is intended to appraise the performance of an individual for supervisory purposes. Rather, the intent of this question, as part of a sport psychology program evaluation plan, is to learn whether program personnel adhered to their roles and responsibilities as delineated in the program design for this particular program (not for their overall professional performance).

* *What things occurred during the program that were not expected?* Once a program has been implemented, it is not surprising to realize that some unexpected things happened. Some of the unforeseen occurrences may be considered positive developments, while others may be seen as negative in nature and scope. Due to these happenings, program implementers may have made adjustments to the program. Answers to this implementation evaluation question will assist you in understanding both these unexpected occurrences and the subsequent program adjustments. This will allow you to make appropriate adjustments to any future implementations of the program.

Table 14.1 lists the above program implementation evaluation questions and provides a chart that you can use in answering each question.

Methods and Procedures for Answering Program Implementation Evaluation Questions

You can employ a range of methods and procedures to answer the implementation evaluation questions presented above. The particular methods and procedures you may use, however, will depend on a range of factors. These factors include the time that is available for gathering implementation evaluation information, the kinds of data that are available to you, and your access to the program and its operations.

Methods and procedures that I have found to be useful for obtaining information to answer implementation evaluation questions include the following:

* Program log.
* Interview(s) with those who are involved with program implementation.
* Program implementation checklist.
* Observation.

Now we will examine each of these methods and procedures in more detail.

Table 14.1 Program implementation evaluation questions

	Yes	No	If no, why not?	Additional comments
To what extent was the sport psychology program implemented according to its design?	(fully)			
Have the components or phases of the program occurred as anticipated?				
Did the intended participants for the program receive the program and participate in it?				
Has the content of the program been covered in an appropriate manner?				
Have methods and materials been used in an appropriate way?				
Have program personnel followed through with their roles and responsibilities with regard to the design of the program?				
What things occurred during the program that were not expected?	(none)			

Program Log

A program log is a method in which a member of the program staff or someone else associated with the program records information about the program and its implementation. As part of the program log method, they may record information about implementation matters such as:

- Notes about each session—how it proceeded and the completion of each session.
- Activities that occurred during the program that were not anticipated and that necessitated adjustments to the program.
- The methods, materials, and content that were used and covered during each program session.
- Changes in the assignments, roles, and responsibilities of program personnel.
- Other relevant program implementation information, given the nature and scope of the particular program.

Interview

The interview method can provide useful information about the program and its implementation. This is especially so if the following conditions exist: (a) rapport and trust have been established between the interviewer and the interviewee; (b) the individual being interviewed is made aware and agrees that the purpose of the interview is to gather information about program implementation; and (c) the interview does not disrupt the operations of the actual sport psychology program and other related programs.

The interview method is best used with those people who are involved in implementing the program. This includes program staff, consultants, and others who have had the opportunity to observe the implementation of the program. During the program implementation interview, the interviewer can ask the individual being interviewed about the following:

- Their opinion about how the program was implemented.
- Aspects of the program that were not implemented as expected.
- Adjustments that were made in the program and the reasons for those adjustments.
- Their satisfaction with how the program occurred.
- Other relevant areas, depending on the program and its nature and scope.

Program Implementation Checklist

A program implementation checklist is a method that contains items related to the program's implementation. This type of checklist is best completed by professionals who actively have been involved in the program and who are familiar with how the program was implemented.

The following items can comprise a program implementation evaluation checklist. You can request that as they consider each of these items, the person completing the checklist should indicate whether each item, in their opinion, occurred as expected (OE) or did not occur as expected (NOE). In addition, they may include qualitative comments for each item as part of the checklist. Items for the checklist include:

- The participants who were supposed to be provided the program actually took part in it.

Table 14.2 Program implementation checklist

	OE	NOE	Qualitative comments
Participants participated Content covered Methods and materials used Roles and responsibilities fulfilled Activities occurred in sequence			

Comments about the implementation of the program:

- The content that was supposed to be covered in the program was covered.
- Methods and materials were used as anticipated.
- Roles and responsibilities were fulfilled.
- Activities occurred in the appropriate sequence.
- Comments about the implementation of the program.

Table 14.2 reflects a chart that you can use for recording information about the implementation of the program.

Observation

The method of observation necessitates that the individual who is observing has been able to spend a substantial amount of time with the program, or otherwise has been embedded in it, while the program was implemented. The observation method can be used effectively if the individual who is the observer has a copy of an evaluable program design. The observer can use that document as an observational guide and look for activities, actions, and other indicators that relate to or involve the implementation of the program.

Communication and Use of Implementation Evaluation Information

Program evaluation implementation information is best communicated as part of an overall program evaluation report. This kind of report may be verbal or written. Chapter 18 of this book will discuss the report in detail.

The most appropriate way to communicate implementation evaluation is to provide the answers to each of your program's implementation evaluation questions, such as those I delineated earlier in this chapter. Along with goal attainment and reaction evaluation information, program implementation evaluation information should be used as a basis for deciding how the program should be designed and implemented if you run it again.

Professional Practice Exercises

1. Describe how you would explain the implementation of a sport psychology program to a director of athletics, including how you would justify resources as a useful expenditure in evaluating the program's implementation.

2. What situations have you or others with whom you have worked experienced when implementing sport psychology programs? How have you or others handled these situations? What would you have done the same or differently in evaluating the implementation of sport psychology programs?

15

EVALUATING GOAL ATTAINMENT

The purpose of this chapter is to provide guidelines for how to conduct an evaluation of goal attainment as part of a program evaluation plan; that is, the chapter overviews how to determine the extent to which the goals of a sport psychology program have been attained. First, the chapter offers relevant context about goal attainment program evaluation, including caveats to consider when undertaking this form of program evaluation. Second, it sets forth a rationale for the importance of goal attainment evaluation of a sport psychology program. Third, it describes the types of goals that may be part of a goal attainment evaluation of a sport psychology program. The last section of the chapter details how to conduct goal attainment evaluations for each of the types of goals. It presents examples of each kind of goal, a key evaluation question related to that goal, and potential methods to use for evaluating that type of goal.

Relevant Context for Goal Attainment Program Evaluation

Goal attainment program evaluation is an important—indeed, a basic—way of gathering evaluative information in order to make judgments about the value of a sport psychology program. This form of program evaluation obtains evaluative information about the extent of attainment of each program goal. This information will allow you to make decisions about the extent to which the goals of the program have been attained.

More specifically, this kind of evaluative information enables judgments about whether each program goal was attained at an expected level, at a less-than-expected level, or at a more-than-expected level of attainment (Kiresuk, Smith, & Cardillo, 1994). For instance, if the sport psychology program goal was "soccer players will apply goal-setting skills for the development of individual mental plans," then the evaluative information allows you to determine the level to which this program goal has been attained.

The task of conducting an evaluation of the attainment of sport psychology program goals has been an essential part of my professional practice. This form of program evaluation has provided me with the discipline to make sure that the goals for the sport psychology programs in which I have been involved are stated clearly to all concerned and that judgments are made about the level or degree of goal attainment.

In addition, goal attainment program evaluation helps me to make sure that sport psychology program goals are based on the needs of program participants. Furthermore, evaluation of program goal attainment allows me to determine if the methods and activities of the program have been linked to each goal and if they have been used in a way that targets goal attainment (Locke & Latham, 2019). Moreover, on more than one occasion, my clients and others who have a stake in sport psychology programs have told me that they have found goal attainment program evaluation very useful to them in understanding sport psychology programming and in determining how to proceed with the program and its goals.

Caveats about Goal Attainment Program Evaluation

I would like to share with you some caveats that are related to goal attainment program evaluation. Recognizing these caveats will assist you in deciding where goal attainment program evaluation fits into the overall sport psychology program evaluation plan. However, misunderstanding, or even dismissal of, these caveats can be detrimental to and limit your program evaluation work and thus negatively affect your professional practice.

The first caveat has to do with the nature of a sport psychology program goal itself. It involves knowing about the methods and activities that are linked to a goal so that program participants can attain that goal. More specifically, if a program goal has been documented—particularly as part of the program's design—and if methods and activities have been implemented to allow program participants to attain that goal, then there is a professional expectation, indeed an ethical one, to evaluate the goal in terms of its attainment. So, for example, if the sport psychology program goal was, "men's basketball players will learn how to use deep breathing during game competition," and if the program contained methods and activities to teach such deep breathing, then you can evaluate this program goal. If you do not accept and act on this professional expectation for goal attainment evaluation, others may question—reasonably so—why the goal was set in the first place.

A second caveat has to do with the situation in which a sport psychology program goal has been set and documented but there have been no methods and activities implemented to assist program participants to attain the stated goal. In this kind of situation, you need to consider whether a goal attainment evaluation should indeed occur at all. This consideration is important because if there were no methods and activities linked to the program goal—even though the goal may have been stated— then the issue arises as to whether it is fair or appropriate to evaluate the program goal.

A third caveat involves a situation where no program goal has been set and documented. In this situation, because there is no stated goal, then it is not defensible to evaluate attainment of it, since the nature and scope of the goal is non-existent. Figure 15.1 is a visual portrayal of these caveats about goal attainment program evaluation.

Rationale for Evaluation of Goal Attainment

The evaluation of goal attainment of a sport psychology program is important for several reasons. First, a sport psychology program can be considered as an investment of resources that have been organized in a systematic manner, preferably by means of an evaluable program design. These resources are an investment in the participants of the program in relation to the stated goals of the program. Therefore, without question, it is a professional imperative to make sure that those goals are considered for evaluation.

Second, and more basically, a goal attainment program evaluation allows you to make judgments about the value of the program for those athletes who have participated in the program. This kind of evaluative information will be helpful in making the case for the continuation of the program, deciding how the program needs to improve, or concluding that the program is best terminated.

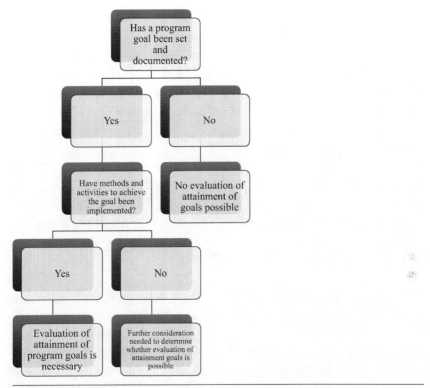

Figure 15.1 Three caveats.

Third, it is important to understand that without an evaluation of the extent to which each sport psychology program goal has been attained, questions about the program's value may arise. It is reasonable to ask the question as to why the program was necessary in the first place, including why resources have been expended on it. Evaluation of goal attainment provides a rationale for the program and the use of its resources.

Finally, the following should be understood: if there have been no goals set and documented for the program, and if no method and activities have been implemented so program participants can attain those goals, then evaluation of goal attainment is not an appropriate form of program evaluation. Otherwise, if such an evaluation were conducted, this may actually result in making judgments about something that really did not happen. In essence, you would be evaluating a "black box," that is, a program in name only, but not one that is evaluable.

Types of Sport Psychology Program Goals

A prior chapter (Chapter 8) covered the task of designing a sport psychology program. In that chapter, I provided an overview of the types of sport psychology program goals that are likely to be part of any particular program. In this chapter, we will review and discuss the types of sport psychology program goals again, now emphasizing the evaluation of the attainment of such goals. This task is important since the types of program goals to be evaluated will determine the kind of program evaluation methods you practically can apply.

From my professional experiences in the practice of sport and performance psychology, I have been involved with the evaluation of many programs. These programs have had many and diverse program goals. The following is a listing and typology of sport psychology program goals that I have set and documented in designing programs and in evaluating goal attainment in relation to those goals:

- *Educational Program Goals* – Educational program goals are established for programs where the program participants are educated or instructed about something that is relevant to their performance or personal development. For example, it may be a goal about becoming knowledgeable about alcohol and drug use policies and procedures of the athletic department, or it may be a program goal about knowing the differences between a growth mindset as opposed to a fixed mindset. Educational goals are not intended to cover mental skills directly. Rather, educational program goals address the acquisition of knowledge or understanding by those who have participated in the program, such as athletes.
- *Mental Skills Program Goals* – Mental skills program goals are set for programs where participants are taught specific mental and emotional skills and are expected to apply those skills before or during actual competition. More specifically, mental and emotional skills are intended to assist program participants in the following ways: (a) helping them prepare for competition; (b) enabling them to compete with a productive mind in the moment presence; and (c) allowing them to deal with the results of their performance in an appropriate way. Mental skills goals reflect competencies such as development of effective routines, breathing and relaxation, energy activation, focus, composure, and accurate self-evaluation.

- *Life Skills Program Goals* – Life skills program goals are set for sport psychology programs that are intended to teach athletes skills that will assist them in developing and maintaining a healthy lifestyle. Life skills program goals are ones that assist athletes with making effective decisions regarding people (e.g., friends and acquaintances), places (e.g., bars and clubs), and things (e.g., alcohol and drugs) that very easily and quickly can put them at risk. The athletes typically encounter these people, places, and things in sport, school, and community settings.
- *Self-Management Skills Program Goals* – Self-management skills program goals are established for programs where athletes are taught how to engage in effective ways to manage themselves, especially outside competitive venues. Typically, programs that have focused on self-management include goals that relate to time management, conflict management, roles and responsibilities management, and information management.
- *Team Development Program Goals* – A team development program goal typically focuses on assisting the team and its members to be an effective team. In this regard, team development program goals reflect knowledge, understanding, and skills that will enable the team to communicate and work together effectively in support of a common cause and in a manner in which they hold themselves mutually accountable.
- *Organizational Development Program Goals* – These are goals for programs that assist organizational leaders, such as mental skills coordinators, coaches, and athletic directors, with the development of policies, procedures, and practices that will assist in the formulation and delivery of programs and services related to the sports for which they hold leadership responsibilities.

The remainder of this chapter provides guidelines for how to conduct goal attainment evaluations for each of these types of sport psychology program goals.

Goal Attainment Evaluation of Educational Program Goals

An educational program goal for a sport psychology program has to do with program participants' understanding. This understanding may involve something like knowing about policies, methods, and procedures that relate to some aspect of their sport. An educational program goal, therefore, also may be referred to as a knowledge goal.

Educational goals are set for sport psychology programs so that participants will learn something and be educated about an important topic or area of performance. An educational program goal, however, is not a mental skills or life skills program goal, since a mental skill or life skill goal addresses a competency to be acquired and demonstrated. (The next sections of the chapter will discuss mental and life skill goals.) For example, an educational goal that is part of a sport psychology program is: "forty-man roster baseball players will learn about the components of the MAC approach to performance enhancement." Note that in this program goal statement, the goal is for the players to become knowledgeable about the MAC approach. It is not for them to be skilled in the application of it, since skill application is another goal.

When conducting an evaluation of the attainment of an educational program goal, the key program evaluation question is: *To what extent have individuals who have participated in the program acquired knowledge that is reflected by the goal statement?*

There are two methods you can use to assess the attainment of educational goals that are part of a sport psychology program, assuming that each program goal has been clearly stated and documented. These methods are:

1. *Pre-Program/Post-Program Assessment Method* – This method develops an assessment questionnaire that incorporates questions that address the educational goal. The program participants are asked to complete the questionnaire before the start of the program. In essence, the assessment questionnaire is intended to measure what program participants know about the educational program goal before the program is implemented. These pre-program responses serve as baseline information about their current level of knowledge with regard to the particular goal.

   Then, once the program is completed, program participants receive the assessment questionnaire again and are requested to complete it again. The responses of program participants from before the program began can be compared to the responses following the program's completion. The differences in responses from pre-program to post-program will determine the extent to which the program participants learned in relation to that educational program goal.

The advantage of this method is that it allows for a comparison of pre-program knowledge and post-program knowledge. A limitation of the method is that it requires the use of the assessment questionnaire at two points in time, which could be problematic for some educational programs to arrange. In addition, this method requires the formulation of an assessment questionnaire.

2. *Post-Program Assessment Method* – This method also develops an assessment questionnaire. This questionnaire is intended to measure the knowledge of program participants as reflected in an educational program goal. The program participants receive the assessment questionnaire to complete at the conclusion of the educational program.

This method does not allow for comparisons of the change in knowledge acquired from before the program; rather, it focuses on what the program participants know following the program. An advantage of this method is that it is given to the program participants only once, at the conclusion of the program. A limitation of this method is that it does not allow for pre-program/post-program comparisons. Here, too, the time and cost incurred in the development of the assessment questionnaire needs to be taken into consideration in deciding how to proceed with the use of this particular method. This saves time and potentially other resources.

Goal Attainment Evaluation of Mental Skills Program Goals

A mental skills program goal refers to the competence that program participants have acquired and have been able to apply, based on their involvement in the program. For example, a mental skills program goal for a program that is designed to assist participants in attaining the goal may be "for players to remain focused on the immediate task at hand during game competition." Another mental skills program goal may be "for players to use deep breathing during game competition." Similarly, a mental skills program goal may be "for athletes to engage in accurate self-evaluation of their performance." These goals go beyond just having knowledge of the skill.

Furthermore, mental skills program goals have relevance during one or more of three separate, interrelated time periods:

1. *Before Competition* – Mental skills associated with preparing for competition (e.g., goal setting, self-talk).
2. *During Competition* – Mental skills associated with competing productively in the moment (e.g., use of the breath, re-focusing, energy activation).
3. *After Competition* – Mental skills involved in accurate evaluation of performance after competition has been completed (e.g., self-evaluation, making adjustments).

Moreover, from my range of professional experiences in sport and performance psychology practice, I have found that mental skills program goals will fall into one of the following mental domains:

- *Perspective* – Balancing the demands of sport and life.
- *Personal Awareness* – Recognizing and accepting current strong points and limitations.
- *Self-Motivation* – Setting and pursuing important and sport-relevant goals.
- *Mental Discipline* – Following through with an effective pre-competition routine.
- *Self-Confidence* – Believing, during actual competition, in the capacity to compete.
- *Emotional Intensity* – Being engaged in competition at an effective level of energy.
- *Focus* – Paying attention to what matters in the moment (e.g., next pitch, next serve).
- *Composure* – Remaining poised in demanding game situations.
- *Teamwork* – Relating productively with teammates and coaches.
- *Self-Esteem* – Keeping oneself as a performer separate from oneself as a person.
- *Performance Accountability* – Being responsible for one's competitive results.
- *Continuous Improvement* – Striving to develop and enhance one's performance and personal development, even despite obstacles.

In conducting a goal attainment evaluation of a mental skills program goal, the key program evaluation question is: *To what extent have the program participants acquired and applied the skill that is explicated in the mental skills program goal?*

There are two methods I have found to be useful and practical in evaluating the attainment of mental skills program goals. These methods are:

1. *Demonstration Method* – This method focuses on having the individuals who are participating in a mental skills program demonstrate a particular mental skill that is incorporated in the mental skills program goal. For instance, if the mental skill being taught is deep breathing, then the evaluator can ask the individual program participant to show (demonstrate) their level of skill to an observer (perhaps you) as part of the program evaluation. The program participant then can be rated as to whether they have demonstrated the skill in a suitable manner. The appropriate use of this method, however, requires that a demonstration assessment method be arranged, either in real time or aided with the use of video.

2. *Application Method* – This method involves assessment of whether and to what extent participants in the mental skills program have been able to apply what they have learned in the program to actual competition. For example, if program participants have been taught how to use deep breathing, the application method would involve getting ratings from those who have observed the athlete in actual competition, such as coaches, sport psychology program consultants, or yourself.

In order for the application evaluation method to be successful, the observers of the program participants need to be willing and able (i.e., trained as necessary) to engage in this form of assessment and to provide feedback about the participants. Gathering of this kind of information can occur at any number of points in time following the completion of the program. The number of times that evaluative information of this nature can be gathered, of course, will depend on the nature and scope of the program as well as the availability of program evaluation resources.

Goal Attainment Evaluation of Life Skills Program Goals

A life skills program goal has to do with acquiring a competency that allows the program participant to make appropriate choices and decisions about factors that influence their lifestyle—factors that may very well place them at risk, particularly with regard to people, places, and things.

A life skills program goal is not an educational program goal or a mental skills program goal; instead, it reflects choices and decisions off the field or outside the competitive venue. Thus, life skills program goals typically have been included as part of sport psychology programs that address the following: (a) relationships of the program participant with other people; (b) frequency of places visited by program participants such as bars and clubs; and (c) use of substances such as alcohol and drugs. Two examples of life skills program goals are "program participants will learn how to cope in an appropriate manner with people, places, and things that can put them at risk" and "program participants will refrain from the use of banned substances."

When conducting an evaluation of a sport psychology program that includes one or more life skills goals, the key evaluation question is: *To what extent have program participants made appropriate choices and decisions with regard to their lifestyles?*

The methods I have found to be practical to use in the goal attainment evaluation of life skills program goals are the following:

1. *Indicator Monitoring Method* – This method involves collecting data on program participants' capacity to remain free of the use of banned substances and any other personal risk indicators. This kind of information can be collected at any number of points of time following the program, depending on the program evaluation resources.
2. *Personal Feedback Method* – This method involves conducting interviews with program participants about how they have dealt with their risk factors, including through discussions of their journals and checklists.

The methods used to evaluate the attainment of life skills goals are advantageous in that the information obtained very well may be helpful to the overall health and well-being of program participants, outside of sport. A disadvantage of this approach, especially with regard to the personal feedback method, is that some athletes (especially student-athletes) may be reluctant to reveal life experiences and their opinions about intimate matters.

Goal Attainment Evaluation of Self-Management Skills Program Goals

A self-management skill program goal reflects a competency of the program participant to manage something that is personal in nature, such as management of their time, conflict, responsibilities, and information. For example, a self-management skills program goal may be, "athletes who have participated in the program will be able to manage the time that they have at their disposal to complete academic assignments." Although self-management skills program goals might be subsumed under other goal areas, such as the life skills or mental skills domains, I have found it useful to have self-management goals listed as a separate type of program goal when I design and implement programs as well as conduct program evaluations.

When conducting a goal attainment evaluation of a self-management skills program goal, the key program evaluation question is: *To what extent have program participants been effective at the management of particular and relevant circumstances?*

There are two methods you can use in a practical manner to gather evaluation information on attainment of self-management program goals. These methods are:

1. *Demonstration of the Skill Method* – This method involves collecting data about how program participants will apply the skill following the completion of the program.
2. *Pre-Program and Post-Program Rating Scale Method* – This method involves participants' completion of a rating scale about their level of competency of the self-management skill.

The advantage of the evaluation of self-management goals is that such outcomes capture information about coping with daily circumstances. A disadvantage is that assessing skill demonstration requires time and resources, as does the use of the rating scale, which necessitates time and resources at two points in time.

Goal Attainment Evaluation of Team Development Program Goals

A team development program goal pertains to an accomplishment of an athletic team or other group (e.g., all pitchers) rather than the accomplishment of individual team members, based on their participation in a team development program. Over my many years of consulting about team development programs, and in designing and implementing them, I have found that the programs that have had value for team members and were sustainable were ones that had clearly stated and meaningful team development goals.

A team development goal may take many forms, depending on the program and its design. For example, a team development goal may be an educational goal such as, "the team will learn about perspectives of being an effective team." Alternatively, a team development goal could be a mental skills goal such as, "the team will interact productively with one another and with coaches, on and off of the field." Yet another example of a team development goal is, "the team has followed through with post-game reviews of their performance as a team."

The key program evaluation question for a team development goal is: *To what extent has the team attained the particular team development goal?*

The methods for gathering information in order to make judgments about the attainment of a team development goal are:

1. *Post-Program Assessment Method* – This method is best used for team educational goals and involves the formulation and use of a questionnaire. It is applied following the program to determine if team members have acquired the information that they were taught, corresponding to the goal statement.

2. *Observation Method* – This method is used for team development mental skills goals. It is used throughout the team development program. It involves observing and then making judgments about the extent to which the team is making progress toward the goal.

3. *Feedback from Coaches Method* – This method is used for team development mental skills and entails interviewing coaches about the team's response to the goal or asking them to provide feedback in another format (such as a brief written report).

Evaluation of team development goals is important. However, it is a form of goal attainment program evaluation that may not be understood by coaches. In this regard, some coaches may perceive the evaluation as being not of the team but as an evaluation of them.

Goal Attainment Evaluation of Organizational Development Goals

In relation to sport psychology programs, an organizational development goal is one that relates to the development and improvement of an athletic department or another sports unit. In this sense, organizational development is identified by indicators such as the following: (a) revision and updating of policies and procedures; (b) communication within the organizational unit or with other entities; and (c) coach and staff education and development. An example of an organizational development goal may be, "head and assistant coaches of all sports have been educated about athlete mental health and their roles and responsibilities." Another example of an organizational development goal may be, "the sports medicine department will update its policies and procedures pertaining to athlete pre-participation assessment."

With regard to the program evaluation of an organizational development goal, a key program evaluation question is: *To what extent has the organization developed in terms of its effectiveness?*

Two methods and procedures for obtaining information about the extent to which organizational development goals have been attained are the following:

1. *Permanent Product Review Method* – This method is used when policies and procedures have been developed. It involves the review of relevant documents and an assessment of their clarity and completeness.

2. *Interviews with Organizational Leaders and Staff Method* – This method is used in order to determine the organizational changes that have been made. It also evaluates how these changes have been integrated into the athletic department or the sports organization.

This type of goal attainment evaluation is advantageous in that it illustrates to organizational leaders the importance of the evaluation of sport psychology programs overall. Its primary limitation can be the time and logistics involved in getting such leaders to participate in evaluation activities.

Figure 15.2 summarizes the types of sport psychology program goals in relation to evaluation questions and methods of goal attainment evaluation.

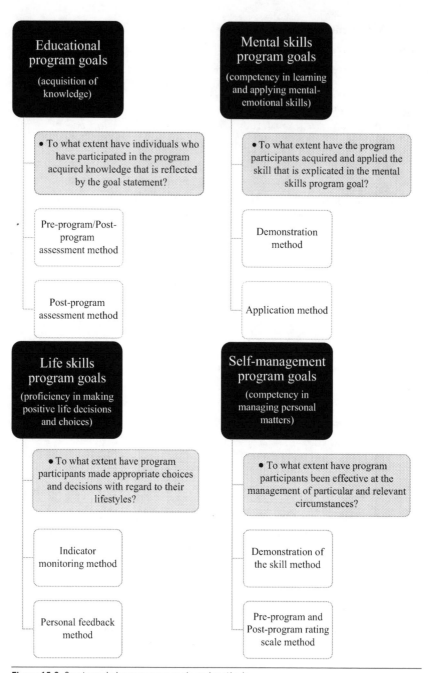

Figure 15.2 Sport psychology program goals and methods.

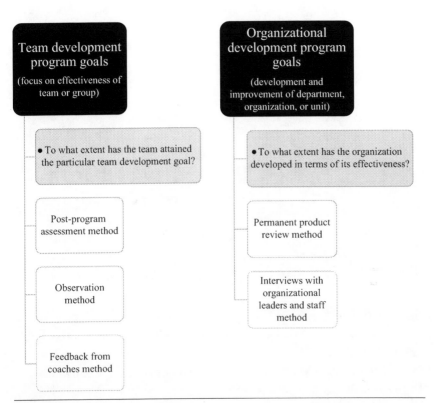

Figure 15.2 Continued

Professional Practice Exercises

1. I and others have found the evaluation of the attainment of sport psychology program goals a challenging task, and sometimes the challenges of this task are not easy to overcome. What have been your experiences in evaluating the attainment of program goals for sport psychology programs? How have you and others dealt with the challenges that arose? What would you have done differently or the same? Why?

2. A coach asks you to tell them whether the team has been attaining its goals. How would you respond to this request?

16
EVALUATING REACTIONS TO THE PROGRAM

The purpose of this chapter is to provide guidelines for obtaining evaluative information regarding the reactions of individuals and groups to the design and implementation of a sport psychology program once the program has concluded, as part of an overall sport psychology program evaluation plan. This kind of evaluation is referred to as a program reaction evaluation. First, the chapter offers a rationale for the importance and usefulness of acquiring information about the thoughts, opinions, and suggestions of program participants and others about the program. Second, it identifies the types of individuals and groups who can be sources for providing program reaction information. Third, it sets forth conditions that are necessary for conducting a program reaction evaluation. Finally, the chapter covers key program reaction evaluation questions and methods that can assist in planning and conducting a program reaction evaluation.

Rationale for a Program Reaction Evaluation

A program reaction evaluation is a particular form of program evaluation. It refers to the process of gathering evaluative information from those who have been involved in the program, both directly and indirectly. The information should be evaluative in nature, as reflected by the thoughts, opinions, judgments, and suggestions of those who are asked to provide their reactions (Patton, 2002).

This form of program evaluation is important because, no matter how large or small in scope it may be, a sport psychology program is an investment of resources. Relatedly, a sport psychology program involves a range of individuals and groups who directly and indirectly are involved in the program and affected by it at all stages—from clarification of the need for the program to its design and implementation—and affected by its program outcomes. These individuals and groups include athletes, coaches, support staff, coordinators, athletic directors, and other executives, as well as those who fund the program. Given the reality of the involvement of many and diverse people in a sport psychology program, obtaining reactions from them about it will provide useful information for making judgments and decisions about the program, including whether and to what extent the program should continue in operation.

Accordingly, program reaction evaluation information reveals the thoughts, opinions, judgments, and suggestions of those who have been involved in the program. More specifically, program reaction evaluation information is important for the following specific reasons:

- Program reaction evaluation information provides those who have had direct and indirect involvement in the program with the opportunity to express their thoughts, opinions, judgments, and suggestions about the program. In my professional practice experiences, program evaluation opportunities of this nature typically provide evaluation participants with a sense of ownership concerning the program; more often than not, they have appreciated the opportunity.
- The information that is generated from a program reaction evaluation complements other kinds of evaluative information that are more quantitative in nature and scope, such as goal attainment program evaluation information.
- Many factors contribute to realization of the outcomes of a sport psychology program, including how the program was designed, how it was implemented, and the extent of participation of those who were involved in the program. Therefore, obtaining reactions from the range of people who have been involved with the program and who have been affected by it also can provide substantial information for making decisions about the program in light of its outcomes.

Sources of Information for a Sport Psychology Program Reaction Evaluation

In any sport psychology program, you can collect program reaction evaluation information from a range of sources (as seen in Figure 16.1). These sources of program reaction evaluation information include, but are not necessarily limited to, the following:

- *Program Participants* – Athletes are the ones who participate directly in most sport psychology programs; therefore, as program participants, they are the most important source of information. They can help you learn how they took part in the program. More specifically, you can seek their reactions to many aspects of the program in which they participated, including: (a) how they were involved in the design of the program; (b) what they consider to have been the program's purpose and goals; (c) what they thought about the program, including what they liked and disliked about it; and (d) whether they believe that the program should be continued for them and/or for other athletes.
- *Program Staff* – You should capture the reactions of the staff who are involved with the implementation of the program. Program staff can be asked about the following: (a) how they were involved in the design of the program; (b) what they consider to be the current strong points and limitations of the program; (c) their use of methods and materials; and (d) their recommendations and suggestions for its continued development and improvement.
- *Coaches and Support Staff* – Coaches, athletic trainers, strength and conditioning specialists, and academic counselors also are valuable sources of information about a sport psychology program, once it is completed. In particular, you can question them about their understanding of the program and its value to them and to program participants, especially with regard to their roles and responsibilities as coaches and support staff members.
- *Athletic Directors, Sports Executives, and Other Relevant Stakeholders* – Although athletic directors, general managers, and performance coordinators have not been involved directly in the program, they do have a part to play in the program due to their oversight of it. This kind of information source also can include those individuals who have provided funding to the program. Thus, learning what athletic

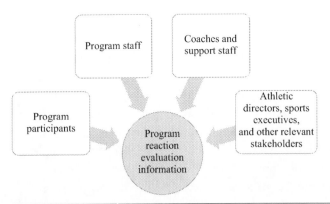

Figure 16.1 Program reaction evaluation information sources.

directors, other sport executives, and program funders understand the program to be in terms of purpose and goals and discovering their opinions about its benefits to program participants will provide useful information. In turn, this reaction information will complement evaluative information obtained from the other sources of information regarding the program.

Necessary Conditions for a Program Reaction Evaluation

Various conditions help as you plan and then carry out a worthwhile program reaction evaluation—that is, an evaluation that results in useful evaluative information for making decisions about the program. The following conditions will contribute to the success of this form of program evaluation:

- There need to be sufficient resources to conduct this form of program evaluation. These resources include the personnel who will be involved in meeting with and interviewing program participants and other program stakeholders. This requires recognition of the availability of the program participants' time and schedules. In addition, funding resources need to be approved for the costs associated with program reaction evaluation activities, such as the formulation of a questionnaire and meeting room rentals.
- Sufficient time and dates must be identified so that those who are going to be asked to provide their reactions to the program—athletes, coaches, others—are available to do so at scheduled times.

- Relatedly, the individuals who are going to provide their reactions about the program need to be informed about the evaluation and their role in it. They also should be apprised of the confidentiality of their responses on a questionnaire as well as during an interview or group meeting. If the responses of information sources are not going to be maintained in confidence, then the evaluation participants need to be notified and given the option to decline to participate in the process.
- The format for the program reaction evaluation, including the development of any questionnaire or rating scale that will be used as part of the evaluation, needs to be clear to all concerned.

Nature and Scope of Program Reaction Evaluation Questions

Some general, overarching program reaction evaluation questions will help you in how to proceed with more specific questions that you will ask those individuals who are serving as evaluation resources. (These more general program reaction evaluation questions are not to be confused with the specific questions that may appear as items on a questionnaire or that are used as part of an interview.) I have found the following general questions to be useful as program reaction evaluation questions:

- What are the reactions of program participants with regard to their involvement in the program?
- How have coaches and athletic support staff understood the program, given their roles and responsibilities with the program?
- How did program staff feel about their experiences in the program?
- What do the athletic director and/or other sports executives think about the program and its value?
- How do others who have a stake in the program view it?

The next sections of this chapter present other, more specific program reaction evaluation questions.

Obtaining Program Reaction Evaluation Information from Program Participants

Most sport psychology programs, whether large or small, target athlete populations. This is the case at professional, collegiate, and secondary school levels. Thus, athletes are the ones who have participated in the program and to whom the program is designed in terms of purpose, goals, and activities.

Without a doubt, it is worth time and effort to obtain detailed information from program participants about their reactions to the program. I have found that you can obtain worthwhile program reaction evaluation information from most athletes who have participated in a sport psychology program by asking them very specific questions.

In my experience, most program participants will respond with useful evaluative information to the following program reaction evaluation questions. These questions, of course, can be customized to align with the nature and scope of your sport psychology program:

- How and when did you learn about the sport psychology program in which you recently participated?
- Was there anything that surprised you when you found out that you were going to participate in the program?
- Were you involved, in any way, in determining the purpose and goals of the program?
- How did you participate in the implementation of the program?
- What about the program did you consider to be interesting and useful to you?
- What about the program did you consider to be uninteresting and not useful to you?
- What have you learned in the program that will make you a better athlete or person?
- What are your suggestions for the continued development of the program?
- Would you recommend participation in this program to other athletes or teams? Why?
- What other comments would you like to share about the program?

Methods to Obtain Program Reaction Evaluation Information from Program Participants

There are several methods you can use so program participants can respond to the above program reaction evaluation questions or to adaptations of them. These methods are:

1. *One-on-One Interview* – For this method, you or another evaluator meets individually with each program participant or a representative sample of individual program participants. As part of this meeting, the participant is asked to respond to the questions listed above as well as to any other relevant questions (depending on the nature and scope of your sport psychology program). This method will provide substantial qualitative information about the participants' reactions to the program. However, you need to allot time for this kind of interview, and each program participant needs to be informed about the confidentiality of their responses.

2. *Focus Group* – This method involves holding a meeting with all of the program participants or with a representative sample of them. At this meeting, facilitated by you or another focus group leader, the program participants focus on some or all of the above program reaction evaluation questions. In this kind of focused discussion, it is likely that common themes across the questions will emerge; these themes should be noted in a summary of the meeting. The focus group method, however, does take planning and time to use. In addition, you need to make clear its purpose to those athletes who are invited to participate, including informing them about how their individual responses will remain confidential.

3. *Open-Ended Questionnaire* – In this method, program participants are provided a questionnaire in either hard copy or electronic format. The above program reaction evaluation questions are included on the questionnaire, and the program participants are asked to comment on each question as they see fit. Here, too, program participants who fill out the questionnaire need to be informed about how their individual responses will remain confidential and will be placed into an aggregate form, with common themes being summarized.

4. *Structured Questionnaire* – This method requires that the program participants respond to a questionnaire that is structured in terms of response format by using a rating scale or another kind of scale. This method probably will take less time to complete by program participants than an open-ended version. However, this method does not allow participants an opportunity to express their thoughts and opinions.

Obtaining Program Reaction Evaluation Information from Coaches and Support Staff

Coaches, athletic trainers, strength and conditioning specialists, and academic counselors are important sources of program reaction information. Even if many of these individuals have not been involved directly in the design or implementation of a sport psychology program, they nevertheless are likely to have reactions to the program. Even if they have only been tangentially involved with the program, or have had no involvement at all, their reactions can provide useful evaluative information.

You can ask coaches and support staff to respond to the following questions, to the best of their knowledge and from their particular perspective:

- To what extent have you been aware of the sport psychology program in which your athletes have participated?
- What are the purposes and goals of the sport psychology program in which your athletes have been involved?
- Have you been satisfied with your level of involvement in the sport psychology program?
- In what ways have your athletes discussed the program with you?
- What do you think are the strong points of the program?
- How do you believe the sport psychology program can be further developed and improved?
- Going forward, what role can you play in the sport psychology program?
- Do you have any other comments about the sport psychology program?

Methods for Obtaining Program Reaction Evaluation Information from Coaches and Support Staff

The methods that are described above for use with program participants also can be used for obtaining program reaction information from coaches and support staff. In this regard, though, I have found the following two methods to be particularly productive in gathering program reaction information from these information sources:

1. *Open-Ended Questionnaire* – This method consists of the formulation of a questionnaire in which the above listed questions are

included; those who fill out the questionnaire are asked to respond to the questions in their own way.

2. *One-on-One Interview* – In this method, all or some of the coaches and support staff members respond in an informal manner to all or some of the above listed questions. In my experience, I have found these individuals to be very comfortable responding in this manner.

Obtaining Program Reaction Evaluation Information from Program Staff

Program staff are those individuals who have been involved with the actual implementation of the program. Accordingly, they are important sources of program reaction evaluation information. They are the ones on the "front line" of the program, and, thus, they need to be approached in a direct but informal manner to learn their thoughts and opinions about the program.

Here are program reaction evaluation questions I have found to be very productive in obtaining evaluative information:

- What were your experiences in being introduced to your role in the program?
- Were the methods and materials that you were asked to use as part of the program practical and productive? If yes, why? If not, why not?
- Did the program proceed in a timely and anticipated manner?
- What were unexpected occurrences that transpired during the program, and how were those situations handled?
- What are your suggestions for program improvement?

Methods for Obtaining Program Reaction Evaluation Information from Program Staff

These program reaction evaluation questions can be addressed by means of the following methods:

1. *One-on-One Meeting* – This method best occurs in an informal way with each program staff member. At the meeting, you use the above questions as a basis for discussion with the program staff member. Using this method, I have found that the individual is willing to share information in a specific way, since the format for discussion is between you and the other party. However, there may be program

staff members who are unable or who do not want to share their thoughts and opinions with you one-on-one.

2. *Group Meeting* – This method is similar to the one-on-one meeting method. The difference is that the questions are used for discussion among all program staff members. A challenge with the use of this method is that staff members may be reluctant to share certain thoughts and viewpoints with the other staff members.

Obtaining Program Reaction Evaluation Information from Athletic Directors, Sport Executives, and Other Relevant Stakeholders

Most athletic directors, general managers, and other stakeholders are not directly involved in a sport psychology program, particularly with regard to its design and implementation. However, this does not mean that they do not have interest in the program. Typically, they may have some knowledge of the program, which may or may not be accurate.

In order to discover this information source's thoughts, opinions, and suggestions about your sport psychology program (once it has been implemented and completed), you can ask them to respond to the following questions:

- What does the area of sport psychology mean to you, given your role?
- What do you know about the sport psychology program that has been implemented?
- What more would you like to learn about the program?
- What other questions or comments do you have about the program?

I have found that the one-on-one interview method is the most productive, in terms of responses to the questions, in obtaining information from this information source in relation to the above listed questions.

Reviewing and Synthesizing Program Reaction Evaluation Information

Based on my experience, once you have obtained program reaction information from the various sources of information, you should find the following process practical and useful in reviewing the information and in looking for common themes across the various groups:

1. Read through the responses of each group, and look for common themes about the program in terms of respondents' thoughts, opinions, judgments, and suggestions, *within each group of respondents*.
2. Next, look for common themes that are prevalent *across each group of respondents*.
3. Then, based on all of the program reaction information, identify the aspects of the program where the reactions seemed to indicate program strong points. Also identify areas where the reactions seem to suggest continued program development and improvement is necessary.

Professional Practice Exercises

1. What have been your experiences with obtaining reactions about a sport psychology program from athletes and others who have participated in the program? What went well, and what did not go so well? Why?
2. What methods of obtaining program evaluation reaction information were most helpful in your circumstance, and why? What were least useful, and why?

17

EVALUATING THE PROGRAM'S STRONG POINTS AND LIMITATIONS

The purpose of this chapter is to provide guidelines for evaluating the strong points and limitations of a sport psychology program once it has been completed, following the review of other program evaluation information. This form of program evaluation—evaluating the program's strong points and limitations—aims to generate evaluative information that can lead to the continued development and improvement of the program. First, the chapter offers a rationale to explain why this kind of program evaluation is important for developing, improving, and sustaining sport psychology programs. Second, it delineates a process that helps you identify and specify elements of the program design that you can evaluate as its current strong points and limitations. Third, it describes and documents a framework for conceptualizing and determining the program's strong points and limitations in relation to those specific program design elements.

Rationale for Evaluating the Strong Points and Limitations of a Sport Psychology Program

A basic and indeed important benefit of conducting a program evaluation is that you are able to determine the strong points and limitations of a sport psychology program (Maher, 2012). Thanks to the evaluation, you can make judgments about the positive features of the program as well as aspects of concern that merit continued development. These decisions are crucial for deciding how to proceed with the program. Without such evaluative information, decisions about the next steps to take with the program may be based on not much more than the opinions of one or two people. Accordingly, evaluating the program's current strong points along with its current limitations serves as a very useful program evaluation task.

More specifically, the task of evaluating the strong points and limitations of a sport psychology program is important—indeed, necessary—for a range of reasons. First, considerable time, effort, and monetary funds are expended on the design and implementation of most, if not all, sport psychology programs. Therefore, those involved with the expenditure of resources expect systematic and thoughtful attention to be given to learning about the elements of the design of the program that are solid and worth keeping as part of the program, as well as to ascertaining the elements that are currently limiting the program's value, especially its value to its participants.

Second, a process is very helpful and truly essential in order to make sense of the program in terms of its strong points and limitations. This process of program evaluation should be practical, should result in useful decision-making information, and should adhere to ethical standards.

Third, when a sport psychology program's strong points and limitations are identified and specified, the resulting evaluative information will be useful in two separate, yet interrelated ways: (1) the information will confirm that one or more elements of the program design needs to continue to be incorporated in the program (i.e., program's strong points); and (2) the information will provide guidance and direction for how the program can be improved going forward (i.e., program's limitations).

Fourth, when you engage in the process of evaluating a sport psychology program's strong points and limitations, you are acting in a highly professional manner. More specifically, you demonstrate your professionalism by showing that you are concerned about the program and how to proceed with it, rather than treating it as a one-time research project.

Process for Evaluating the Strong Points and Limitations of a Sport Psychology Program

A systematic process will help to ensure the generation of useful decision-making information as you seek to evaluate the strong points and limitations of a sport psychology program. Toward that end, consider the following process that I have used and found to be very helpful (once the program is completed) for making sense of the value of a program in terms of its strong points and limitations:

- *Define a Program Strong Point* – A sport psychology program strong point is an element of the program's design that the generated evaluative information, such as information from goal attainment evaluation and program reaction evaluation information, has judged to be valuable. Subsequently, you can consider this program design element a strong point that should continue to be part of the program if the program is implemented again.
- *Define a Program Limitation* – A sport psychology program limitation is an element of the program design that has been judged as not valuable to the program; thus, it requires revision and improvement if the program is going to continue. A decision needs to be made about what to do with the limitation: to remove it from the design of the program or to improve it.
- *Identify the Program Design Elements* – In order to make judgments about whether an element of the program design is a strong point or limitation, you need to identify specific program design elements. The identified elements serve as the reference points from which judgments can be made. The following are program design elements that are worth judging as either a program strong point or a program limitation, respectively:
  - *Participation in the program* – The athletes participated in the program in a meaningful way (strong point), or participation in the program was inconsistent and did not meet expectations (limitation).
  - *Purpose and goals of the program* – The purpose and goals of the program were clear, or they were vague, misunderstood, or not even recognized.
  - *Sequence and timing of program activities* – Each of the activities of the program were seen as an important part of the program, or there were activities that were considered unnecessary.
  - *Application of program methods and materials* – The methods and materials of the program were applied in an effective way, or they were not applied as expected or not used at all.

- *Location and facilities for the program* – The program's location and facilities contributed to the program, or they limited the implementation of the program.
- *Dates and times of the program* – The program occurred on days and times that were convenient, or the days and times of the program were seen as a hindrance.
- *Quality of the instruction in the program* – The instruction was considered meaningful, or it was considered meaningless.
- *Other program design elements* – (Your judgment here depends on the nature and scope of the program.)
- *Obtain Information about the Program Design Elements* – In order to make judgments about the strong points and limitations of a sport psychology program, you should base your judgment on trustworthy information. Thus, it is necessary to review and evaluate information such as the following:
  - Records of program attendance.
  - Information about how the program was implemented: this will be available if a program implementation evaluation was conducted.
  - Information about the extent to which goals of the program have been attained: this will be available if a program goal attainment evaluation was conducted.
  - Program reaction evaluation information: this will be available if a program reaction evaluation was conducted.
  - Comments from those who have been active in the implementation of the program, including athletes, program staff, consultants, and program participants.
  - Your own observations of the program, in light of your role in it.
  - Other relevant information, depending on the nature and scope of the program.
- *Make Judgments about the Program* – Based on the information you have obtained and reviewed about the program, you will be ready to make judgments about whether each particular program design element was a strong point or a limitation. During this step, you analyze each program design element, and, with the information you have at your disposal, you consider the indicators associated with each program design element.

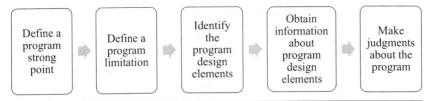

Figure 17.1 Process for determining the value of a program in terms of its strong points and limitations.

Figure 17.1 is a visual portrayal of the process for determining the value of a program in terms of its strong points and limitations.

Framework for Conceptualizing and Determining the Program's Strong Points and Limitations

The remaining sections of this chapter describe the indicators for each program design element. What follows, therefore, are indicators that I have found to be helpful in making judgments about the strong points and limitations for particular program design elements of a sport psychology program.

Participation in the Program

The degree of participation in a sport psychology program is relevant in considering how to proceed with its continued development. This program design element can be considered as a strong point or limitation using the following indicators:

- The rate of attendance of participants during the program.
- Reactions by participants who have taken part in the program.
- Level of motivation and effort manifested and reported by program participants during the program.

Purpose and Goals of the Program

It is important to consider this program design element, since the purpose and goals of a program can determine what happens to the program following its implementation. Here are some useful indicators for determining the program's strong points and limitations related to purposes and goals:

- The reason why the program has been designed is clear to program participants.
- The goals of the program are specific and measurable, and program participants, staff, and other relevant stakeholders understand them.
- The goals are relevant to program participants with regard to their mental and emotional development and performance.
- Appropriate evaluations determined that the degree of the attainment of the program goals was at expected or more-than-expected levels.

Sequence and Timing of Program Activities

How a program is implemented—in terms of the sequence and timing of the activities of the program—can very well influence how the program is implemented in the future and the extent to which it should continue. Here are indicators to consider for this program design element:

- The activities occurred when they were scheduled.
- It was clear what activities were to occur and when.
- The individuals who were responsible for the activities followed through with them.

Application of Program Methods and Materials

Very good indicators for this program design element are the following:

- The methods and materials that were expected to be used during the program were used as expected.
- Program participants were engaged with the methods and materials.
- Unexpected methods and materials were used.

Location and Facilities for the Program

The location and facilities for the program can be important contributors to the program and, consequently, they may be strong points or limitations. Here are some useful indicators for this program design element:

- The location for the program was convenient and readily accessible for program participants and staff.
- The facilities were clean and conducive to instruction and learning.
- The facilities were ready at the beginning of the program.

Dates and Times of the Program

The days on which a program is scheduled as well as the times when it is supposed to occur can influence how the program is implemented and whether it can sustain itself. In this regard, the following are appropriate indicators for this program design element:

- The dates and times scheduled for the program were convenient for program participants and program staff.
- The dates and times for the program were clear and made known to program participants and staff prior to the implementation of the program.

Quality of the Instruction in the Program

Some sport psychology programs have an instructional emphasis. For those types of programs, here are some indicators to use in order to make judgments about the strong points and limitations of the program:

- Program participants were attentive and engaged in the instructional process.
- The instruction provided was linked to the purpose and goals of the program.
- Instruction was adapted to the needs of program participants, based on evidence, during the program.

Table 17.1 provides a sample chart for helping determine whether program design elements are strong points or limitations.

Professional Practice Exercises

1. Think about how you and others have made judgments in the past about the strong points and limitations of sport psychology programs in which you have participated or otherwise been involved. What were these evaluation experiences like? How could they have been modified or improved?
2. If a head coach asked you right now to explain how a mental skills program in which their athletes had participated could be improved, how would you respond to the coach's request? Why?

Table 17.1 Judging program design elements

	Strong point	Limitation
Participation	The athletes participated in the program in a meaningful way.	Participation in the program was inconsistent and did not meet expectations.
Purpose and goals	The purpose and goals of the program were clear.	Purpose and goals were vague, misunderstood, or not even recognized.
Sequence and timing of program activities	Each of the activities of the program was seen as an important part of the program.	There were activities that were considered unnecessary.
Application of methods and materials	The methods and materials of the program were applied in an effective way.	The methods and materials were not applied as expected or not used at all.
Location and facilities for the program	The program's location and facilities contributed to the program.	The program's location and facilities limited the implementation of the program.
Dates and times of the program	The program occurred on days and times that were convenient.	The days and times of the program were seen as a hindrance.
Quality of the instruction	The instruction was considered meaningful.	The instruction was considered meaningless.
Other design elements		

18

COMMUNICATING AND USING PROGRAM EVALUATION INFORMATION

The purpose of this chapter is to provide guidelines for communicating and using the evaluation information that has been generated about a sport psychology program once the program has been completed. First, the chapter offers a rationale for why purposeful and precise attention needs to be given to the communication of program evaluation information; it also explains why those responsible for the program's continued development should be involved in the analysis of the information. Second, it describes and discusses the tasks necessary for the successful communication and use of program evaluation, including the formulation of a program evaluation report.

Rationale for the Communication and Use of Program Evaluation Information

The communication and use of program evaluation information by those who are responsible for the sport psychology program are essential activities of the process of developing and sustaining such programs. Regrettably, though, these activities often are neglected. Without successful follow-through with the activities of communication and use of program evaluation information, the entire process of program development can be called into question (Stufflebeam, Madaus, & Kellaghan, 2000). However, the successful completion of these activities increases the likelihood that actions will be taken for the continued development and improvement of the program.

Within this context, *communication* of program evaluation information means conveying results about the program to carefully targeted audiences who have responsibility and a stake in the program. This communication may be in written as well as in verbal forms. Typically, a program evaluation report serves as a very good medium for communicating program evaluation information.

The *use* of program evaluation information refers to the following: (a) purposefully involving coaches, program staff, athletic administrators, and others in reviewing program evaluation information; (b) considering what the information means to them with regard to the program; and (c) deciding the program development actions to take to further develop and improve the program.

Tasks for Communicating and Using Program Evaluation Information

There are several tasks that, if successfully completed, will contribute to the effective communication and use of program evaluation information. These tasks are:

- Formulate a program evaluation report.
- Target the audiences for the receipt of program evaluation information.
- Specify the evaluation information that is to be communicated to the target audiences, including how, by whom, and when the information will be communicated.
- Involve the target audiences in the review and use of the program evaluation information.
- Pinpoint program development actions, the roles and responsibilities for taking these actions, and additional feedback.

Each of these tasks will now be discussed in the remaining sections of this chapter (visually portrayed as Figure 18.1).

Formulating a Program Evaluation Report

A program evaluation report is a written document intended to provide information about the program to those who need it, particularly your client and other relevant stakeholders. The report should not be an overly detailed

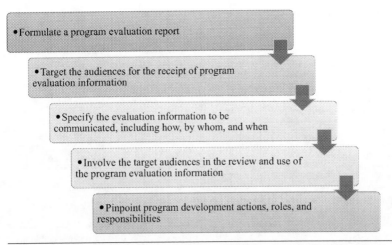

- Formulate a program evaluation report
- Target the audiences for the receipt of program evaluation information
- Specify the evaluation information to be communicated, including how, by whom, and when
- Involve the target audiences in the review and use of the program evaluation information
- Pinpoint program development actions, roles, and responsibilities

Figure 18.1 Tasks for effective communication and use of program evaluation information.

or technical document. Rather, it should be used as a basis for communication with your client and other relevant stakeholders.

Furthermore, you can customize or otherwise add to a generic report based on the interests and needs of those who will receive the report. For instance, I have found the following template very useful in formulating a program evaluation report:

I. Title of the program – This title should be the same as that used in the program design.

II. Individual(s) who conducted the program evaluation.

III. Purpose of the program evaluation – To provide evaluation information about the program as a basis for the program's continuous development and improvement in the organization.

IV. Program participants – Demographic and other relevant information on the athletes or others who have participated in the program.

V. Description of the program – Program purpose and goals; program methods, procedures, and activities; program staff; and other relevant information.

VI. Program evaluation questions and results.

Table 18.1 Program evaluation report checklist sample

	Yes	No	Comments
Title of program	X		
Individual(s) who conducted the program evaluation	X		
Purpose of the program	X		
Program participants	X		Specify by team
Program description		X	Get from files
Program evaluation questions & results	X		
Actions, roles, and responsibilities for development and improvement	X		
Appendices		X	Add consent forms

    A. How was the program implemented in relation to its program design?
    B. To what extent have the goals of the program been attained?
    C. What have been the reactions of those who have been involved in and with the program?
    D. What are the current strong points and limitations of the program?
  VII. Actions, roles, and responsibilities for the continued development and improvement of the program.
  VIII. Appendices – Includes evaluation forms and instruments and other relevant material, such as informed consent forms.

Table 18.1A provides an example of a sport psychology program evaluation report, while Table 18.1 provides a sample of a program evaluation report checklist.

Targeting the Audiences for Receipt of Program Evaluation Information

To successfully accomplish this task, you first identify the individuals or groups who expect to receive or otherwise should receive program evaluation information. In essence, these target audiences are the individuals and groups who are affected by the program; that is, they have a stake in the program. In

Table 18.1A Example of a program evaluation report: Summary only

Title of the program	Mental Skill Development Program for Collegiate Student-Athletes
Individuals who conducted the program evaluation	Licensed sport psychologist, as part of their services contract with the university Mental performance coach, employed by the athletic department of the university
Purpose of the program	To provide program participants with knowledge so that they can develop their mental skills in relation to their roles on their respective teams, and so that they can apply these skills during competition.
Program participants (n=28)	10 members of the women's basketball team 12 members of the men's basketball team 6 members of the women's tennis team
Description of the program	Goals of the program: (1) Learn mental skills for developing effective pre-game routines, and for maintaining focus and composure during competition; (2) Apply the mental skills they learned before and during competition. The program was organized by the following components: (a) pre-program assessment of mental skills knowledge; (b) mental skills group instructional meetings; (c) follow-up sessions to discuss application of mental skills. The program occurred over a six-month period, beginning in August and ending in February, with one group meeting every two weeks during that time frame.
Program evaluation questions and results	*Who participated in the program?* Of the possible 28 participants, all of them were involved in all the group instructional meetings, while 18 of the 28 participated in one-on-one meetings. *How was the program implemented?* The program was implemented according to its design for the most part: Group instructional sessions were held as scheduled for most of them; scheduling adjustments had to be made for some sessions, due to weather and changes in practice times. This affected the number of student-athletes who could participate in the one-on-one meetings.

(continued)

Table 18.1A (Cont.)

Title of the program	Mental Skill Development Program for Collegiate Student-Athletes
	In what were the participants instructed? The participants learned how to develop a pre-game routine using a routine tracker checklist. They learned how to use the MAC approach for focus and paying attention to what matters in the moment, and they learned how to use deep breathing and self-talk for coping with competitive pressure. *What did the participants learn and apply?* Based on pre-program interviews and reaction surveys, 26 of the 28 participants reported they learned mental skills methods they previously did not know. Of the 28 participants, 18 of them were able to demonstrate what mental skills they were able to apply during actual competitive situations.
Actions for continued development and improvement	Based on participant reaction survey information, provide more flexible days and times so that program participants can be involved in one-on-one meetings. Provide the head coaches with more timely and specific information about the content of instruction and getting their feedback on their observations of their student-athletes.

addition, some of them may be able to contribute to the continued development of the program with such information.

Besides yourself, there are a range of individuals who can be targets for communication of program evaluation information and who should receive a program evaluation report. These individuals include the following:

- Your client.
- Athletic directors or other sports executives who oversee the program.
- The staff who have been involved in implementing the program.
- Those who supervise the staff who have implemented the program.
- Program participants.
- Those who have funded the design and implementation of the program.

Once you have identified the target audiences for program evaluation information, I recommend you specify how each of these individuals or groups are likely to contribute to the program going forward.

Examples of contributions include the following:

- They can assist in the revision or addition to one or more program design elements.
- They can help with marketing the program.
- They are able to authorize funds for the continuation of the program as well as for its expansion to other settings.
- They can endorse the program.
- Other contributions, depending on the nature and scope of the sport psychology program.

Specifying How Program Evaluation Information Will Be Communicated

Once you have identified the target audiences for the program evaluation information, you need to decide what information needs to be communicated. Toward this end, the program evaluation information chart, seen as Table 18.2, has proven to be a useful tool.

As you use this table and as you decide how to proceed with the communication of program evaluation information, the following definitions apply:

- *Target Audiences* – The individuals who will be provided with program evaluation information.
- *Nature of the Information* – This information may be reflected by a program evaluation report that you already have formulated. If not,

Table 18.2 Example of program evaluation information chart

Target audience	Director of sports medicine	Executive director of athletics
Nature of evaluation information	Report about the Mental Skills Development Program for student-athletes	Copies of the program evaluation instruments and evaluable program design
How to communicate the evaluation information	Written summary report	One-hour meeting to review and discuss the program and next steps with it
Communicators of the evaluation information	Sport psychology consultant	Mental performance coach
Time frame for communication of the evaluation information	One month following the completion of the program	

the information to be communicated may be in the form of program summary or overview.

- *How to Communicate* – This refers to whether a program report or a summary should be provided in advance of a meeting with the target audiences or whether there will be a verbal discussion at a meeting.
- *Communicator* – The one who will provide the information and follow up on it.
- *Timeframe for Communication* – The dates and times for delivery of written information or for meetings.

Involving Target Audiences in the Use of the Evaluation Information

If the target audiences are going to receive information from the program evaluation, then it stands to reason that they should be involved in the review and use of the information they have received. The target audiences' involvement with the program evaluation information is not an end unto itself. Rather, the intention is to have them utilize the information so they can contribute to the continued development and improvement of the program and so the program can sustain itself over the course of time.

In this regard, I have found the Program Evaluation Planning Meeting a productive way to involve target audiences in the use of program evaluation information. This method endeavors to involve the client and other relevant stakeholders in the consideration of the program evaluation information. It also urges them to use this information as a basis for pinpointing actions that can lead to the continued development and improvement of the program.

You can employ this method successfully by doing the following:

1. Set a date, time, and location for the meeting with you, your client, and other relevant stakeholders.
2. Prior to the meeting, provide these individuals with information about the program evaluation. This may be in the form of a report, tables, or a list of main points from the program evaluation.
3. Request that the individuals who have received this information review it prior to the scheduled meeting. Ask them to note specific questions, thoughts, and concerns that they would like to discuss at the meeting.

4. At the meeting, you and they review the results of the program evaluation and discuss the information. The intention of the meeting is to obtain feedback from your client and from the others who will attend the meeting about what actions can be taken so that—if the program is going to be continued—the likelihood increases that the program will be sustained as a valuable one going forward.

Pinpointing Program Development Actions, Roles, and Responsibilities

Once the program evaluation information has been communicated to the target audiences, and following their involvement in analyzing the results of the information, you now are ready to take specific program development actions. These actions are ones that, if taken, should improve the chances that the sport psychology program will be further developed so it can continue to be implemented in the organization. You will be attempting to pinpoint particular development actions, roles, and responsibilities that will enhance the program as it moves forward.

Here is a listing of program development actions that may need to be taken, based on program evaluation information:

- Revisions in program eligibility criteria for program participants.
- Alterations in the nature, scope, or substance of the purpose and goals of the program.
- Content changes.
- Revisions in methods, materials, or activities.
- Changes in location or facilities.
- Resequencing or changing of the timing of program components, phases, or activities.
- Revisions in program policies and procedures.
- Modifications in roles, responsibilities, and relationships of program staff.
- Budget requests or alterations.
- Other program development actions, depending on the nature and scope of the particular program.

For each and every program development action, you need to document the following:

Table 18.3 Example of a program evaluation action chart

Program improvement actions	Determine why program participants were not willing or able to attend the one-on-one meetings that were a component of the program. Decide how coaches of the teams that will participate in future versions of the program can be informed about the participation and progress of their athletes, within the context of ethical guidelines.
Responsibilities for the actions	Mental Performance Coach in conjunction with the Director of Sports Medicine.
Time frame to follow through with the actions	To occur during the summer (July–August).
Accomplishment of the improvement actions	Written communication to the Sport Psychology Consultant and the Executive Director of Athletics.
Rationale for the actions	The program has value for its implementation with other student-athletes. Therefore, addressing and resolving the action will result in an improved version of the program.

- The rationale for the action.
- The individuals who need to be involved to ensure that the specific action is authorized, sanctioned, implemented, and accomplished.
- The time frame for the action to be accomplished.
- The evidence that will indicate that the action has been accomplished.

I have found Table 18.3 to be helpful in making sure that program development actions are documented and accomplished.

Professional Practice Exercises

1. What have you found to be the most meaningful means of providing program evaluation information to your clients?
2. Ask coaches, athletic directors, and other sport psychology program stakeholders what they would like to learn from a program evaluation report. If they have had the opportunity to review such reports in the past, find out what they liked or disliked about them. What do their responses mean to you with regard to your communication and use of program evaluation information?

19

CLOSING COMMENTS AND PROGRAM DEVELOPMENT PRACTICE STANDARDS

This book has been created as a resource guide for practitioners who are involved in the development of sport psychology programs in real-time settings at professional, collegiate, and other levels of competitive sport.

The chapters of the book have included recommendations and suggestions that can assist practitioners, including you, with successfully addressing important program development activities, from clarifying the need for a sport psychology program to focusing on details regarding program design, implementation, and evaluation. Much of the information covered in this book has come from my many years of experience as a practitioner at the professional, collegiate, and other levels of sport. The principles of program planning and evaluation presented in this book have informed and guided my professional experiences.

In closing, I would like to share the framework I have used to make sense of my program development work in sport and performance psychology. The framework is focused on four standards that I have upheld as part of my reflective practice. These standards reflect the following ethical norms:

- *Practicality* – The practitioner assists clients and others in a way that focuses, in a systematic and practical manner, on the needs and contexts of those individuals and groups who have been involved with the program design and implementation.

- *Utility* – The practitioner works to provide timely and meaningful information to clients and others. This information contributes to the design, implementation, and evaluation of sport psychology programs, in the service of making those programs an integral part of the organization.
- *Propriety* – The practitioner adheres to ethical and legal standards related to the clarification of need and context, along with the design, implementation, and evaluation of sport psychology programs.
- *Technical Appropriateness* – As part of the sport psychology program development process, the practitioner employs methods, procedures, and instruments that are valid and reliable for the purposes for which they were intended.

I hope that you will find these standards to be useful as you proceed to assist your clients and others with developing and sustaining sport psychology programs in your particular role within your own work setting.

APPENDIX A
EXAMPLE OF A PROGRAM DESIGN

Mental Performance Rehabilitation Program for Professional Baseball Players

Relevant Context

The mental and emotional development of our players in relation to their performance has been a longstanding and ongoing organizational commitment at all levels of the organization. This includes those players who are involved in the physical rehabilitation process at the Development Complex, and it is for these players that the Mental Performance Rehabilitation Program for Professional Baseball Players (hereafter referred to as Program) is intended.

Program Participants

The participants in the Program are manifold with different injuries and recovery time frames. It is expected that there will be around 30 players with injuries at the onset of the program. The number will continuously vary as the season progresses and players move to and from affiliates. As the season progresses, it is anticipated that more players will enter the group while other players will leave it as they complete their rehabilitation.

Program Personnel

- *Mental Performance Coaches* will facilitate the Program and be responsible for group and one-on-one sessions.
- *Coaches and Support Staff* will be encouraged to observe and provide their thoughts and opinions during the sessions and throughout the overall program. Coaches and support staff will also facilitate the development of any goals or routines discussed in the sessions.

Purpose and Goals of the Program

The purpose of the Program is to support those players who are going through the rehabilitation process so that they can continue to learn to use their thoughts, emotions, and actions effectively during their physical rehabilitation experiences.

As a result of their participation in the Program, the players are expected to make progress toward the following goals:

1. Learn how to spend purposeful and productive time on their mental game during their rehabilitation process (i.e., on the development and refinement of their thoughts, emotions, and actions as a baseball player and person).
2. Become increasingly skilled at quality preparation—being mentally and emotionally ready to rehabilitate day by day—through the formulation and use of effective routines, coupled with purposeful deep practice, as this skill pertains to their return to play and their particular individual physical rehabilitation plans.
3. Become consistently skilled at self-motivation—setting and pursuing important goals—so they are able to focus on the process of their individual rehabilitation plans.
4. Become skilled at being honest with themselves as they are working on their continued rehabilitation and improvement.
5. Enhance their self-confidence in relation to an effective rehabilitation process by learning how to incorporate imagery into their daily work.

Components of the Program

In order to assist the players in attaining the above goals, the Program has been organized around three components: (1) Meetings with Players in Groups of Five or Fewer (in English and Spanish); (2) One-on-One Player

Mental Performance Support; and (3) Communication and Collaboration with Rehab Support Staff.

Component 1: Small Group Meetings

This component of the Program will encompass no more than seven small group meetings for each small group of players (five to eight in a group) who are involved in the rehabilitation process at the Development Complex. Two mental performance coaches will lead these small meetings in English and Spanish. In order to assist the players who will be participating in the Program to make progress toward the goals that have been described in the prior section of this program design, the group meetings will be scheduled during the time periods when the mental performance coaches are on site. In small groups, the players will be involved in discussion of a range of topics delineated below. (We recognize that the focus of some topics may change, based on particular circumstances and exigencies.)

The mental domains and topics for the small group meetings are:

1. *Teamwork* – Interacting productively with other players and with rehab staff. Players will discuss accepting their roles, assuming responsibilities, and developing productive relationships. This mental domain will be addressed during small group meetings one, four, and seven.

2. *Perspective* – Keeping things in balance—baseball and life. This allows players to discuss how to separate out themselves as a person from themselves as a performer during their time in rehab. Their personal sides will be the focus here: getting the players to understand their value as a person and their vision as players. It also addresses learning how to cope with risk—people, places, things (including states such as boredom). This mental domain will be covered in session two.

3. *Self-Motivation* – Pursuing SMART goals with enthusiasm and effort. During the third small group meeting, the notion of looking for and recognizing "small daily wins" will be discussed. Mental goal-setting discussion and activities will center on:
   • Specifying the mental goals that will allow the player to commit to and follow through in an effective manner on their rehabilitation experiences (S).

- Formulating a procedure so that progress toward the mental goal(s) can be monitored and measured, preferably through multiple methods (M).
- To the best extent possible, making sure that the players' mental goal(s) can be attained by the player, given their overall natural characteristics (A).
- Determining how the attainment of each mental goal will be relevant to the player's continued development and performance (R).
- Developing a time frame when it is appropriate to measure progress and when it is likely that progress toward the mental goal(s) will be made (T).

4. *Composure* – Being able to cope in an effective way with the demands encountered during physical rehabilitation. Understanding the MAC framework will allow players going through the rehabilitation process to embrace the recovery process and stay focused in their day-to-day activities. This will be achieved by players being able to discuss the benefits of having their mind in the moment (M), accepting the experience (A), and committing to the recovery process (C). This mental domain will be covered in session five.

5. *Self-Confidence* – Believing in the capacity to rehabilitate. Players will experience evidence-based imagery procedures to learn how they can increase levels of confidence in the rehabilitation process. Visualization techniques assist in maintaining functional components of baseball-related skills and healing imagery to decrease rehabilitation time. This mental domain will be covered in sessions three, four, and six.

6. *Mental Discipline* – Following through with a plan and making necessary adjustments, including work on the field, given their rehab plans. This meeting will address the present obstacles and roadblocks the players are coping with during the rehab process. Additionally, it will cover the development of healthy routines that will allow the players going through rehab to cope with adversity. This mental domain will be covered in session seven.

Component 2: One-on-One Player Mental Performance Support

Based on the information covered and discussed in the small group meetings, players are likely to have questions and matters on which they would like to receive assistance and discuss further. Toward that end, players will be encouraged to seek out external guidance from mental performance coaches for the Program to address any additional concerns. This may involve work with the player, both on the field or in other locations at the complex.

Component 3: Communication and Collaboration with Rehabilitation Support Staff

In order to better serve our players, the mental performance coaches will collaborate with the physical rehabilitation support staff in order to provide the opportunity to create individualized plans that offer relevant information to the players. The collaboration with the physical rehabilitation staff will occur throughout the program in order to provide a consistent message for the players, given where each player is within the rehab process and in conjunction with their rehab plans.

Program Evaluation

The program evaluation plan will focus on the answering the following questions using multiple methods of data collection (which will be described in the program evaluation plan):

- Who participated in the Program, in terms of relevant demographic and baseball-related characteristics?
- How was the Program implemented in terms of what went well and what did not proceed as expected?
- What were the reactions of players and staff to the Program?
- What did players learn as a result of their participation in the Program?
- What have players applied in rehab and non-rehab settings, based on what they have learned during the Program?
- What are the next steps in the continued development of the Program?

A program evaluation report will be provided to player development and front office staff.

APPENDIX B
SPORT PSYCHOLOGY PROGRAM EVALUATION PLAN

Purpose of the Program Evaluation

- Provide the Director of Athletics and Head Coaches of the respective teams with information about how participating student-athletes benefitted from the program and how the program can be further implemented and approved.
- The sport psychology program consultant will be responsible for the formulation and implementation of the program evaluation plan.

Description of the Program Design (Overview)

- There are expected to be 28 program participants (10 members of the women's basketball team; 12 members of the men's basketball team; and 6 members of the women's tennis team).
- Goals of the program are: (1) learn mental skills for developing effective pre-game routines and for maintaining focus and composure during competition; and (2) apply the mental skills that they have learned before and during competition.
- The program will be organized by the following components: (a) pre-program assessment of mental skills knowledge; (b) mental skills group instructional meetings; and (c) follow-up sessions to discuss application of the mental skills.

- The program will occur over a six-month period, beginning in August and ending in February, with one group instructional meeting occurring every two weeks during that time frame.
- The instructors for the program will be two mental performance coaches contracted with the athletic department.

Program Evaluation Questions and Protocols

1. *Who participated in the program?*
   - Data will be gathered from program attendance and participation logs.
   - Data will be analyzed in terms of the percent of participants from each team who attended the sessions and who followed through with assignments.
   - The mental performance coaches will be responsible for the data maintenance and collection.
   - Results will be used to help decide the practicality of the program.

2. *How was the program implemented?*
   - Data will be gathered by means of a review of the logs that document the activities that will occur as the program is implemented.
   - There also will be behavioral observations made of a random sample of group instructional sessions.
   - Data will be analyzed by comparing what was expected to occur as part of the program design and what actually occurred.
   - The mental performance coaches will be responsible for the maintenance of the implementation logs.
   - The behavioral observations will be conducted by the sport psychology program consultant.
   - The data will be used in determining whether the program can be reasonably implemented again with other student-athletes and teams.

3. *In what were the participants instructed?*
   - Data will be gathered from a review of the implementation logs.
   - Data will be analyzed by the means of documenting the content of instruction that has occurred in relation to the program goals to which the instruction was related.

- The sport psychology program consultant will be responsible for this form of data collection.
- The data will be used in deciding if the program focused on the mental skills that were identified during the needs assessment (which occurred at an earlier time).

4. *What did the participants learn and apply?*
   - Data will be analyzed in terms of the pre-program interviews with program participants and on program reaction survey results.
   - Data will be analyzed in terms of the percent of student-athletes who reported that they have learned specific mental skills based on their responses to a mental skills checklist.
   - Data also will be analyzed by means of interviews with a random sample of participants with the focus being on how and when they applied the mental skills as well as obstacles faced in trying to apply them during competition.
   - The sport psychology program consultant will be responsible for the data collection.
   - The data will be used in deciding the value of the program for the participants and whether and to what extent the program should be implemented and approved.

Confidentiality and Ethical Matters

- Program participants will be informed about the plan for program evaluation, and they will sign an informed consent document.
- Data that will be reported will only be in aggregate form, whereby the identities of individual participants will not be revealed.

Program Evaluation Budget

- The costs associated with the program evaluation will be reflected as part of the contracts of the sport psychology program consultant and the two mental performance coaches.

REFERENCES

American Educational Research Association, American Psychological Association, & National Council of Measurement in Education. (2014). *Standards for educational and psychological testing*. Washington, DC: Joint Commission on Standards for Educational and Psychological Testing.

Aoyagi, M. W., & Portenga, S. T. (2010). The role of positive ethics and virtues in the context of sport and performance psychology. *Professional Psychology: Research and Practice, 41,* 253–259. doi:10.1037/a0019483

Brown, C. H., Gould, D., & Foster, S. (2015). A framework for developing contextual intelligence. *The Sport Psychologist, 19,* 51–62. doi:10.1123/tsp.19.1.51

Checkland, P. (1999). *Systems theory, systems practice.* Hoboken, NJ: Wiley.

Clauss-Ehlers, C. S., Chiriboga, D. A., Hunter, S. J., Roysircar, G., & Tummala-Narra, P. (2019). APA multicultural guidelines executive summary: Ecological approach to context, identity, and intersectionality. *American Psychologist, 74,* 232–244. doi:10.1037/amp0000382

Damschroder, L. J., Aron, D. C., Keith, R. E., Kirsh, S. R., Alexander, J. A., & Lowery, J. C. (2009). Fostering implementation of health services research findings into practice: A consolidated framework for advancing implementation science. *Implementation Science, 4,* 50. doi:10.1186/1748-5908-4-50

Durlak, J. A., & DuPre, E. P. (2008). Implementation matters: A review of research on the influence of implementation on program outcomes and the factors affecting implementation. *American Journal of Community Psychology, 41,* 327–350. doi: 10.1007/s10464-008-9165-0

Fletcher, D., & Wagstaff, C. R. D. (2009). Organizational psychology in elite sport: Its emergence, application, and future. *Psychology of Sport and Exercise, 10,* 422–434. doi:10.1016/j.psychsport.2009.03.009

Forman, S. G. (2015). *Implementation of mental health programs in schools: A change agent's guide.* Washington, DC: American Psychological Association.

Fried, E. J., & Flake, J. K. (2018). Measurement matters. *Association for Psychological Science, 31,* 29–30. www.psychologicalscience.org/observer/measurement-matters

Heath, C., & Heath, D. (2007). *Made to stick: Why some ideas survive and others die.* New York: Random House.

183

Joint Commission on Standards for Educational Evaluation. (1994). *The program evaluation standards: How to assess evaluation of educational programs.* Thousand Oaks, CA: Sage.

Kane, M. T. (2013). Validating the interpretations and use of test scores. *Journal of Educational Measurement, 50,* 1–73. doi:10.1111/jedm.12000

Kaufman, R. (2000). *Mega planning: Practical tools for organizational success.* Thousand Oaks, CA: Sage.

Keegan, R. (2015). *Being a sport psychologist.* London: Palgrave Macmillan.

Kiresuk, T. J., Smith, A., & Cardillo, J. E. (Eds.). (1994). *Goal attainment scaling: Applications, theory, and measurement.* Hillsdale, NJ: Lawrence Erlbaum.

Locke, E. A., & Latham, G. P. (2002). Building a practically useful theory of goal setting and task motivation. *American Psychologist, 57,* 705–717. doi:10.1037//0003-066X.57.9.705

Locke, E. A., & Latham, G. P. (2019). The development of goal setting theory: A half century perspective. *Motivation Science, 5,* 93–105. doi:10.1037/mot0000127

Maher, C. A. (2011). *The complete mental game of baseball: Taking charge of the process, on and off the field.* Bloomington, IN: Authorhouse.

Maher, C. A. (2012). *Planning and evaluating human services programs: A resource guide for practitioners.* Bloomington, IN: Authorhouse.

Maher, C. A. (2018). Simplexity and baseball: Keeping the game simple, within its complexity. *The Baseball Observer, 10,* 30–32. https://view.joomag.com/mag/0379012001491973480?feature=archive

Maher, C. A., & Taylor, J. (2015). Do you have a watering can? Cultivating your clients. In J. Taylor (Ed.), *Practice development in sport and performance psychology* (pp. 143–158). Morgantown, WV: Fitness Information Technology.

Maxwell, J. C. (2014). *Good leaders ask great questions: Your foundation for successful leadership.* New York: Center Street.

McCarthy, P. (2019). Goal setting. In A. Mugford & J. G. Cremades (Eds.), *Sport, exercise, and performance psychology: Theories and applications* (pp. 221–232). New York: Routledge.

McEwan, D., & Beauchamp, M. R. (2014). Teamwork in sport: A theoretical and integrative review. *International Review of Sport and Exercise Psychology, 7,* 229–250. doi:10.1080/1750984X.2014.932423

Patton, M. Q. (2002). *Qualitative evaluation and research methods* (3rd ed.). Newbury Park, CA: Sage.

Poczwardowski, A., & Sherman, C. P. (2011). Revisions to the sport psychology service delivery (SPSD) heuristic: Explorations with experienced consultants. *The Sport Psychologist, 25,* 511–537. doi:10.1123/tsp.25.4.511

Raaen, G., & Mugford, A. (2019). Working with organizations in sport, exercise and performance psychology. In A. Mugford & J. G. Cremades (Eds.), *Sport, exercise, and performance psychology: Theories and applications* (pp. 75–85). New York: Routledge.

Sharp, L., & Hodge, K. (2011). Sport psychology consulting effectiveness: The sport psychology consultant's perspective. *Journal of Applied Sport Psychology, 23,* 360–376. doi:10.1080/10413200.2011.583619

Stufflebeam, D. L., Madaus, G. F., & Kellaghan, T. (Eds.). (2000). *Evaluation models: Viewpoints on educational and human services evaluation.* Boston, MA: Kluwer.

Taylor, J. (2008). Prepare to succeed: Private consulting in applied sport psychology. *Journal of Clinical Sport Psychology, 2,* 160–177. doi:10.1123/jcsp.2.2.160

Wagstaff, C. R. D. (Ed.). (2017). *The organizational psychology of sport: Key issues and practical applications.* New York: Routledge.

Weinberg, R. (2010). Making goals effective: A primer for coaches. *Journal of Sport Psychology in Action, 1,* 57–65. doi:10.1080/21520704.2010.513411

INDEX

Printed in the United States
by Baker & Taylor Publisher Services